# An UNSUSPECTING Child

Coming to Grips with Covert Childhood Abuse

*An*
# UNSUSPECTING
*Child*

MARYLEE MARTIN

ARCHWAY
PUBLISHING

Archway Publishing books may be ordered through booksellers or by contacting:

Archway Publishing
1663 Liberty Drive
Bloomington, IN 47403
www.archwaypublishing.com
844-669-3957

ISBN: 978-1-6657-0839-5 (sc)
ISBN: 978-1-6657-0838-8 (hc)
ISBN: 978-1-6657-0840-1 (e)

Library of Congress Control Number: 2021912259

Print information available on the last page.

Archway Publishing rev. date: 10/8/2021

For my daughter, a woman of substance,
who urged me to tell my story.

For all the little ones who can't.

# Preface

*Who is an unsuspecting child? Probably most of us, in one way or* another. We are born an innocent bundle of love, expecting and trusting the adults who care for us to keep us safe. And then sometimes our lives change abruptly, unexpectedly, due to the choices made and paths taken by those same adults. Maybe our stability gets rocked when Dad or Mom accepts a job in a new state, and we have to move, leaving our home, our friends, and our relatives behind, and our entire sense of security slides out the door with the furniture. Maybe our parents go through a divorce, and the new life without one of our parents leaves a hole we don't know how to fill. Maybe we are sent to a religious school, private school, or public school, depending on our family's religious beliefs or net worth, and our way of seeing the world is shaped by that decision. As we mature into adulthood, we take what we've been taught and make some rules of our own that we break as we learn about life.

Sometimes adults make decisions that affect children in terrible ways. The overt act of abusing a child sexually or physically can cause lifelong effects of devastation. There is a third type of abuse, rarely talked about, that also changes a child's life forever. Known as covert sexual abuse, it often occurs in dysfunctional families where a parent needs to replace the emotional ties that they are missing due to alienation from a spouse. Because of the lack of hands-on action, those of us who have experienced it are often dismissed. "It that even a real thing?" I was once asked. "Why can't you just forget it?" Living through the mental trauma of covert abuse is difficult and may take a lifetime to overcome. Some of us become alcoholics, prostitutes, or drug addicts. We find ourselves acting out and making awful decisions. We ultimately survive, but the damage we cause ourselves along the way extracts its own steep toll.

I've made many mistakes in my life. It took me a long time to realize that it wasn't enough for me to know how things had happened. The more important question was why? I had to go back in time to discover the seeds that had begun with the generation before me and had grown into a troubled lifestyle that I didn't understand, couldn't seem to control, and lived in the dark with for most of my adult life. In the wake of the courageous #MeToo movement, which has shed light on the pervasiveness of sexual harassment and abuse, there must also be an opportunity for those of us who were unsuspecting children when tragedy struck to say #WeeToo—"wee" for the little ones.

I was an unsuspecting child, and this is my story.

# One

*My mother grew up in an orphanage.*

Her mother, Leona, was a gentle, stoic, and deeply religious Catholic. She didn't smile much when I knew her, but her life had been difficult; she had been abandoned by a husband who had left her with five small children and no way to take care of them. She never talked about it, and we were not allowed to ask. Some things were simply not discussed.

Grandma Leona, whose family had emigrated from Prussia, was the tenth of thirteen children. Her father had lost his first wife during the birth of their fifth child. Leona's mother had married him six months after the death of his wife, and they had gone on to have eight more children of their own. Leona was a sweet, happy girl; she was smart and creative and loved to write stories. In any family photo, she stands out among all the children for her curly brown hair and large dark eyes. Though she had older brothers and sisters, it was Leona who was pulled from school at fourteen to stay home and help raise her three younger siblings. It's unknown why she was chosen, but she did as she was told. Grown-ups made the rules, and children followed them.

Leona was in charge of baking the daily bread and rolls from scratch; helping to make soap from boiled scraps of fat, ashes, and lye; cleaning the kerosene lamps; beating the carpets; and carrying buckets of water into the house from the pump outside, all while watching the little ones. To the delight of her siblings, Leona learned to make homemade apple butter and ice cream. She must have had mixed feelings about going from being a child in school one day to taking care of a house the next, yet despite all the new responsibilities, Leona continued writing her stories and homeschooled herself by reading every chance she got. My mother said it was Leona's faith in God that gave her the strength to do everything she did. It was a good thing she had that strength, because she was going to need it.

My grandfather Frank was the tenth of fourteen children. He came from a long line of Bosnians who had eventually settled in Illinois. His father, John, was highly respected in the field of agriculture. John had the foresight to hold on to his property during tough times, and over the years he enlarged it immensely. He enlisted the help of his five sons and ended up on easy street. Those sons, including Frank, reaped the rewards of their father's foresight. Farming was their life, and it supported them extremely well. John attributed his success to the teachings of the Catholic Church. He retired from farm life in the 1920s and invested in the stock market. He was living the good life until the stock market crashed in 1929 and the Depression hit. He lost an enormous amount of money but kept his faith.

Frank was dashingly handsome and was permitted to attend the Christian Brothers College in St. Louis, Missouri, where he earned a law degree. He was full of energy and enthusiasm and life. He had gone to college, something no one in the family had ever done. Being a good son, he returned to the farm with his law degree and did what he could to guide the family. With Frank's tall, dark, eye-catching looks and Leona's striking appearance, it seemed only natural they would find each other. And there were additional perks: Leona already knew how to take care of a home and children, which made her ideal wife material, and Frank had unlimited potential as a provider. They were married October 16, 1917. They had only seven months together before Frank was drafted in May 1918. At the time, Leona was pregnant with their first child and worried about her husband. But Frank's service lasted only a year. He fell ill during the Spanish flu pandemic, which infected five hundred million people and killed fifty million. Frank was one of the lucky ones who survived. He was honorably discharged and returned home.

Frank had entered the service full of vitality but came out weak and exhausted. When he finally recovered, he and Leona moved to a large farm in Freeburg, Illinois, where they had several hired hands to help with the work. Leona took care of the small, one-story redbrick house, once again pumping water for laundry and cooking. They had five children in quick succession—four girls and a boy. She birthed her fourth child alone at the farmhouse while Frank rushed for the doctor. My mother, Milly, was second-oldest. What had seemed like an ideal start to a happy life must have soured for Frank as his responsibilities grew greater. Months after their fifth child was born, Frank sold the farm and separated from Leona, leaving her with the children and no support.

I never learned what became of Frank after he left my grandmother. No one talked about it. But no one ever talked about anything in my family. Leona, jobless and facing the prospect of raising five small children on her own, made a difficult decision: she moved the baby in with her cousin and sent the four older children to an orphanage while she went to work. The lives of these unsuspecting children would change forever because my grandfather took a self-serving path. It was a decision that would affect all our lives.

# Two

*What should have been an idyllic childhood on a sprawling farm with* a loving family was completely upended during my mother's formative years as she was forced into a situation over which she had no control. The Guardian Angel Home in Joliet, Illinois, was run by the Sisters of St. Francis of Mary Immaculate. The sisters had been called to their work by an act of God. One morning in 1864, at High Mass, a thunderbolt had struck the steeple of the church, traveled to the ground, and resulted in the death of five people. One of those killed was the mother of three. Her husband was devastated and asked the sisters to care for the two youngest children. Over the next thirty-two years, the sisters took in and cared for hundreds of orphaned and needy children. As their charges grew, they built a larger facility on the Fox Estate, a former mansion, renovating it and other buildings on the premises to house their orphanage.

There, they cared for up to three hundred children at one time. In choosing a name, they were adamant that the word "Home" be used to reflect their desire to foster a "homelike atmosphere." They included "Guardian Angel" to remind them that this would be a model Christian family. Although the idea was noble, home and family were things my mother must have missed terribly.

Mom told us only a few stories about her time in the orphanage. On the night she and her siblings arrived, the three girls were sent to one side of the building, and my uncle was sent to the other. Mom and her older sister managed to sneak down to the garden and meet up with their little brother. They sat together and hugged each other until they were discovered and promptly sent back to their respective dormitories.

Mom spent seven years at the orphanage, from the age of six to thirteen. Seven years is a long time for a child to develop a sense of herself, her family, and her outlook on life. But other than saying she received a great education, no matter how much we begged her for details, my mother would not discuss those years. None of her siblings would talk about the experience either; perhaps they'd made a pact to keep it to themselves. I believe it would have helped my mother if she had opened up about it; it would have helped us all.

What was it like for her during the days and nights of those years? Did she feel abandoned by both her parents? Was she frightened? Did she live separated from her sisters, or were they at least allowed the comfort of one another? Did she get to see her siblings when they played outside? Did she have any friends to confide in? How often did Grandma come to see them? Did she get hugs and kisses? Was she safe? Did anyone hurt her?

So many unanswered questions. Why wouldn't she talk about it? This much was clear: those years affected her mind in a way that laid a path for our future.

Grandma Leona made good use of her time without her children. She worked a series of jobs as a beautician, food-service employee, hotel maid, and Walgreens counter girl while sleeping in small apartments above a bakery where she also worked. She saved her money, and in July 1933, she went back to the orphanage to get her kids.

Leona made a home for her children in an apartment in Peoria, Illinois. In 1937 the family moved to St. Louis, Missouri, where her brother and sisters also had settled. It isn't difficult to imagine how hard her life was back then as a single mother of five, but she persevered. Grandma never remarried after Grandpa left. She was Catholic and therefore did not believe in divorce. We never met our grandfather. We never heard from him. He did not write or send postcards. To my knowledge my mother never saw him again. I remember that she received a check when he died, but she gave half of the money to me and half to my sister, taking none for herself. She wanted no part of him.

Mom was a tough cookie. If you could get her to laugh, you had really achieved something. She always had an inner conversation going that none of us could hear. She was fiery and strong, and sometimes that fire bubbled up into rage. At other times, she was the sweetest, most elegant woman in the room. But she was never not troubled.

In St. Louis, Mom met Dad.

# Three

*My father, Ray, was the second of five children. The world he grew up* in was completely different from the one my mother lived in. He was the favorite son in a tight-knit family. Dad's mom, Mary Catherine, came from a long line of English immigrants and was the fourth of twelve children. His father, John, came from Irish immigrants. John was the third of ten children. They were obviously dedicated and devout Catholics. But above all else, John's family was Irish. Even though Grandma Mary Catherine was English, and Mom was French and German, according to Dad, we were Irish. It never occurred to us that we might be anything else, and on this point, Mom never argued with him. When I was twelve, I sang "Tri Colored Ribbon" in a competition at an Irish Feis and won second place. I loved being up on the stage alone, lost in a song that made my father so happy. The first-place finisher was an elderly man who played "Danny Boy" on the bagpipes.

Like my grandmother Leona, Mary Catherine also was pulled out of school by her parents. It's interesting how often that happened in those days. However, Mary Catherine grew up in Clearfield, Pennsylvania, in a nice home in a flourishing middle-class family. She was largely responsible for raising her two younger brothers, a toddler sister, and an infant sister. Mary Catherine was the nanny, and she took it seriously, so seriously that we didn't call her Grandma; we called her Nanny. When she finally got a job as a clerk outside of the home, she was thrilled. "I have a dandy position at Leitzinger's Store," she'd say. Mary Catherine was an easygoing yet strong woman who adored her siblings, but she must have been thrilled to be out in the world without them.

In 1914, Mary Catherine met her future husband, John, and wrote to her uncle that she had "suddenly fallen in love with a mighty nice man. He's good, sober, Catholic, and in the Knights of Columbus." What more could a woman want? John worked as a trainman for the New York Central Railroad. They married and lived in Clearfield, Pennsylvania, until 1916, when they had their first child, Genevieve. Soon after, the family moved to Akron, Ohio, where John went to work making tires at B. F. Goodrich for five dollars a day. There was no union at the time, but in 1932 the American Federation of Labor came to Goodrich, and things improved. John served as the treasurer of Local #5 at B. F. Goodrich until June 1, 1953, when he retired. By executive board and membership approval, John was given a lifetime pension. He was Local #5's only pensioner. John and Mary Catherine had been married for forty-three years when John died of a heart attack.

Ray, my dad, was the second of five children born to

John and Mary Catherine. Dad was handsome. He had a lot of girlfriends and a passion for life. He loved going to parties and picnics and having cookouts, as well as going ice skating and taking walks. Once, he and his siblings held a funeral for a dead mouse that he'd found, actually stopping traffic to carry it across the street. Most of the time, Genevieve, Ray, and their friends spent evenings listening to records and making popcorn. He and his older sister were the closest of the siblings, but they all considered themselves a tight group and defended each other more often than they squabbled. Those were the fun days, before the heartache of World War II.

In 1939, Hitler invaded Poland, England declared war on Germany, and America was two years away from joining the Allies. Ray chose to enlist in the Army Air Force (as it was known back then) rather than wait to have his name pulled from a goldfish bowl for the draft. My father was stationed at Jefferson Barracks in St. Louis, Missouri. That was where he met Milly, my mother.

My father and some of the other soldiers noticed a poster for a USO dance and decided to go. Mom and her sister went too. As Mom told it, all the girls were on one side of the dance floor, and all the "fellows" stood on the other side. When the music started, there was a rush of uniforms across the floor, and Mom, who was very short, thought, *Oh, I hope that tall guy isn't going to ask me to dance!* Of course, he did.

Dad told it a bit differently: "Once I got a look at your mom's great-looking gams, I wasn't about to let her go. She was the prettiest girl in the room." (Many years later, while suffering from Alzheimer's, Mom would say that they met at a UFO dance. If they were introduced by aliens, it would explain so much about my family.)

My parents fell in love, mostly through letters as he moved

from base to base, especially when he was stationed in Guam. Dad worked there repairing fighter planes that were going back and forth to Japan. He lost many friends during that time, when they flew away and never returned. Mom and Dad married while Dad was still in the service. Mom tried to meet up with him when she could, but he was in high demand repairing airplanes, and she waited patiently for her love to return.

When he was discharged, Dad took Mom home to Ohio and his family. Dad's brother and sisters were all fashionable, intelligent, and deeply connected. The entire clan was very reminiscent of the Kennedys in spirit, but without all that bothersome money. Friends, laughter, and family commitment were everything. More importantly, they were Irish, which meant they were the best of the best. Mom was from St. Louis and wasn't Irish. She was not a member of the inner circle. I give her great credit for having the courage to leave home to follow the man she loved, but I'm certain she was not counting on the loneliness she felt, being so far away from her family and stuck in the midst of this tight-knit group. After everything she'd been through growing up, she had enough self-doubt to last a lifetime. Yet she became a dedicated homemaker to two small children and her "Charlton Heston–handsome husband." But things would not remain peaceful. Over time, their backgrounds would collide, causing problems for them both.

*The firstborn child in my family was my sister Kathy. She was a pretty* little girl with dark curly hair, huge brown eyes, and freckles. I'm sure Dad was happy, but I'm also sure he would have loved a son. Mom wanted a red-haired son. I came out blonde with green eyes, so there would be no red hair or boys for them.

Kathy is five years older than I am, and we had little in common even as children. Those five years were a large gap. I always felt like an only child as my sister sped through school, skipping a grade and making her way into the world seemingly without effort, while I muddled my way through, lost in a haze. We looked nothing alike, thought differently, acted differently, and were not really friends. We did, however, fight with tenacity. We were sisters.

Our family played Scrabble and Monopoly together and did puzzles on the kitchen table. We ate meals together. We were regular people in an ordinary, all-white town, and we lived in a safe bubble of our own little world. Sometimes our parents argued. Mom had a bad temper, and Dad tried to keep things calm, but it wasn't easy; she had a short fuse. We didn't eat meat on Friday, and we went to confession on Saturday and Mass every Sunday. Kathy and I played in the backyard and lay in the grass watching the ants. We sat on the front porch steps and waited for the ice cream truck, listening for the musical tinkle so we could run inside and ask Mom for two dimes for popsicles. Then we'd sit on the steps and suck the sweet juice from the ice. Often, we were on our own until dinner; Kathy was with her friends, and I was with mine. For the most part, we were normal kids from a normal family. At least, that's how we appeared from the outside.

I made my television debut at age four on a TV show called *Charming Children*, broadcast from WXEL Studios in Parma, Ohio. Much like *Sesame Street*, it was designed for small children to learn and have fun. And did we ever have fun on that set! We heard stories, danced, and were made to feel important. I'm sure I thought I was one of the *most* charming children. This was the beginning of my relying on a very active imagination, which would eventually save my sanity.

When things got too tense around the house, I would disappear into my room, pull out my collection of Disney records, and sing into my hairbrush. I would become the heroine of every Disney movie, and then I felt safe.

Mom loved music. There was always music in our house. Dad bought Mom a piano for their fifth anniversary, and she loved to play for us. My sister began lessons when she was young, and she was quite talented for her age. I could peck out a few notes, but I didn't have the discipline to practice like Kathy did. Mom told me, "You'll regret it one day when you can't play," but no one could ever tell me anything. She was right. I *do* regret that I can't play. I still peck at the keys.

I began to take dance lessons at five. That I could do! I'm pretty sure that's where my love of the stage began. As our recital piece for the Charles Boyd Studio, we did a routine to the song "Hickory, Dickory, Dock," dressed as mice in pink tutus with long, fuzzy gray tails, headbands with gray fuzzy ears, and ballet slippers sprayed silver. None of the other little girls could remember the steps, so Mr. Boyd pulled me out in front of the line so that the others could watch my feet. That's probably when it happened: alone out there onstage, five years old with the crowd all to myself, lost in the darkness, the lights, the music, and the dance. I was in my own magical world. When the music stopped, and I heard the applause and cheering, I'd almost forgotten the other kids were there. I was sure all the applause was for me.

*There were supposed to be three girls in our family. I was five and a half* when my baby sister was delivered full-term but stillborn on December 27, 1955. My sister's death changed our lives so dramatically that our family never recovered from it.

My little sister was a Rhesus (Rh) factor baby. About 85 percent of us have the Rh factor in our red blood cells, making us Rh-positive; 15 percent of us lack the Rh marker and are thus Rh-negative. The Rh factor doesn't become a problem unless the mother is Rh-negative, and the father is Rh-positive. The incompatibility of these two factors can cause jaundice, anemia, or in severe cases, stillbirth. With today's medical science, doctors can perform blood transfusions while a baby is still in utero, and immunizations are available against the Rh marker during pregnancy. But this wasn't true in my sister's time. My mother was inconsolable.

They named her Mildred Mary after my mother and the Blessed Virgin.

Mom was in the hospital for five days. During that time, my well-meaning aunts—my dad's sisters—came to our house and completely disassembled the baby's room. They got rid of her clothes, her crib, and anything that would remind my mother of the baby she had lost. When my mother did eventually come home, she saw the empty room and cried. I believe that part of her grieving process for her lost child would have involved slowly boxing up the baby clothes and cleaning out the room. But she was robbed of that opportunity and left with nothing.

I used to sit in church with my mom and dad and Kathy and fold my hands and pray that God would perform a miracle and bring my baby sister back. I knew about miracles. God could do it. There was a large stained-glass window on the wall behind the altar, and sunlight would shine through it. Every Sunday, I begged God to open the window and bring my little sister floating down on that light into my mother's arms, to make her and our whole family happy again. I knew He could make it happen; He was God.

I prayed and prayed and prayed, but nothing happened. I think that's when I stopped believing in miracles.

Mom took care of the house. A perfectionist, she kept our house spotless. She did the cooking, the cleaning, the sewing (man, could she darn socks!), the laundry, the ironing, the canning of jellies, and everything else a woman was expected to do in those days. She had a large flower garden in the backyard, and she pulled weeds with a fury. She made us lookalike clothes for special occasions (I liked the swing skirts with the poodles on them) and supervised our prayers at night. But Mom and I weren't close. She wasn't a hugger or a kisser; she was a yeller, and she had such a temper that it scared me. I, of course, was too young to be told about or to comprehend the complexities of her upbringing that contributed to these behaviors.

Daddy could do anything. He was good with his hands, and our basement was filled with saws and tools and electrical equipment. He spent his time repairing radios and TVs, record players, and lights. He taught my sister how to use a soldering gun, and she used to love to hang out in the basement with him, learning to do it all by herself. Dad also loved to build things: decorative cabinets, clocks, shelves, and stands and even a patio and, once, a garage near our first house. He could land-scape, and he repaved our driveway. In the eyes of his children, he was a hero. Plus, Daddy was nice and kind, and he never yelled.

Daddy also liked me best, as my sister would be the first to tell you. Dad was a talented amateur photographer, and he had his own dark room in the basement. I liked to go down there and watch the pictures coming to life, like magic, in the developing fluid. Dad had a calendar with a naked picture of Marilyn Monroe on it. Mom caught me looking at it one day and ripped it down and threw it away. Dad mourned the loss of that calendar for years. He took photographs of flowers and birds, portraits of family, and close-ups of hands. "You can tell a lot about a person by their hands," he would say. He entered his photos in local camera club contests.

Dad was always taking pictures of me. His camera was there to capture every shiny curl, every laugh, every smile, every mood. His younger daughter was beautiful, or so he told any-one who would listen. There were pictures of me everywhere. There was one at his office, on the mantle, and a huge one centered on the wall in the living room that had been entered in one of those photography contests. There were a few pictures of my sister but not as many, and they weren't as big. Sometimes she didn't like me very much. All those pictures didn't help.

My father wasn't telling the truth, of course; I wasn't that pretty. By the time I was six, my blonde curls had changed to a dullish light brown, and I was quite ordinary. But not to my dad! I was his beauty. I went off to grade school with this lie in my head. I had been told that I was the "special one," the "perfect one," and the "one God blessed" him with. In school, though, I wasn't much of anything.

I wasn't cute or popular. I could have been smarter, but I never could seem to apply myself. I was always lost in my head. My sister was brilliant, and because she had skipped a grade, she would graduate high school at sixteen. "You are Kathy's sister, right?" the nuns asked. "You can do better."

My parents' marriage became more and more volatile as time passed. Mom's depression grew after Mildred Mary's death, and her short temper continued to get shorter. Dad stopped being able to console her and became more distant. They grew further and further apart.

That was when I started getting headaches. I was six years old, and Mom called them my "sick headaches." I'd be throwing up, and Mom would turn out all the lights in my room and put a cold washcloth on my head. I just wanted everything to be quiet while I cried myself to sleep. Back then, we didn't know about the effects of stress on a child.

My mom's grief and my father's sadness filled our house every day. Had my older sister and I been close, we could have turned to each other for comfort, but we didn't. We were living separate lives together. It took us until adulthood to discover how much we loved the two girls who had taken such different paths as children.

My sister hated all the attention I got. One day, she was

singing upstairs in her room when our father came up and told her to "stop that croaking." She was crushed. My sister had and continues to have a lilting soprano voice; she's even a cantor in her church. But back then, it meant nothing. Her straight As didn't get her the praise and attention she deserved. I never saw the damage that was being done to her all those years as she was cast aside. Instead, I basked in all the attention. I was Daddy's favorite, and I played it for all it was worth.

Our house was full of tension. Mom was always mad about everything. If a glass broke, she'd get mad. If someone spilled milk, Mom got mad. But every now and then, Mom seemed happy, and I wanted to keep that going, so I'd do anything she wanted just to keep the peace. I'd jump if she told me to do something, or I'd try to make her laugh. I'd make Dad laugh just to keep him happy so that Mom in turn would be happy. There were times when Kathy and I would come home from school and pause before going in the door because we never knew if we were going to get "happy" or "mad" Mom when we went inside. But Kathy was my mother's girl and loved Mom unconditionally. Kathy was always there for her and defended her no matter what was happening. I was Daddy's girl. We'd each chosen our side.

# ix

*Just before I started school, we moved to a bigger house in the pristine* city of Cuyahoga Falls with its manicured lawns and tree-lined streets. The lawns were perfect, due not to landscapers but to hardworking fathers and kids earning money. The house had a screened-in porch with a swing hanging invitingly. Mom had Dad plant lilac vines on one side. When they bloomed, the fragrance would drift across the porch while we played or read. Kathy and I had our own rooms. And Mom got a fresh start in a new house where there weren't so many sad memories.

Dad went to work at a car dealership. Until about the age of six, I thought we were wealthy. Dad brought home a brand-new car every year, right off of the line and a top-selling model. My sister finally said, "Of course, we get a new car. They give salesmen a demo car to drive, dummy!"

Dad's position as a top seller at the dealership had its perks.

One time we were asked to do a print ad for Ford, arranged through my father's company. We were supposed to be having a picnic, a new Ford parked near us. Mom had my sister and me in cute dresses. There was another family scheduled for the shoot too, and that mom showed up with her daughter and son in shorts. The ad people felt that her kids looked more like they were going on a picnic than we did, so they used that family, and we were out. Thanks, Mom. You lost our ad to a woman with a better sense of playwear.

We walked to school every day, jumped rope, and played hopscotch. Though Kathy and I each had friends from school to play with, if there was no one else around, we would watch *The Mickey Mouse Club* on TV together or play cards or board games. The problem was that my sister had the advantage of age. She won all the games and bossed me around. I tried to keep up, following in her shadow. Sometimes, we were just keeping out of trouble. We could find common ground when we were avoiding Mom's temper. We played school on the front porch, and Kathy got to be the teacher, of course. She'd make up lessons for me and make me take tests, which she graded. I hated playing school. I hated going to school. As often as I could, I'd hop on my bike and ride two blocks to my friend Yvonne's house, where we'd sit and talk or play records, watch TV, and laugh a lot.

Mom would tell me to be home by a certain time to get ready for dinner, and I was never late. Mom always wore a housedress, as women did in those days—even when she was cleaning or ironing or washing the floor! Kathy and I did the dishes every night. She would wash, and I would dry, singing in harmony at the top of our lungs. Mom and Dad loved watching *The Lawrence Welk Show*, and we loved the Lennon Sisters. They sang a song called "Tonight You Belong to Me," in harmony and repetition, and Kathy and I chose that as our favorite doing-dishes song. Those were great times because of the one thing we had in common: we loved to sing! We had chores to do every day and cleaning on Saturday, but Mom always made sure we had time to play. Maybe she enjoyed the freedom of having us out of her hair. Summers were the best, though, because we could swim in the town pool and see our friends.

One summer afternoon when I was eight, I walked over to Yvonne's. I don't know why I didn't ride my bike. Maybe Mom had given me some cookies to share, which would not have been unusual, and I couldn't ride my bike and carry the cookies at the same time. Anyway, Yvonne and I played our games and laughed as we always did, and I left for home at my pre-appointed time. No one wanted to make Mom mad by being late. Never, ever get Mom mad: that was the rule.

I had gotten only a few feet from my friend's house when a man in a car pulled up next to me very slowly, rolled down his window, and asked for directions. "Excuse me," he said. "I'm not from around here. Do you think you could tell me how to get to State Road?"

It was an easy question. Everybody knew how to get to State Road. I started to answer. Then I remembered I wasn't allowed to talk to strangers. So I shut my mouth and kept walking.

He slowly drove along beside me. "I know you go down to Sackett Street and turn. I just don't know if it's left or right."

It was left. *Should I tell him?* All I had to do was say "left." "It's left," I said.

"Oh, thanks. Then what?" he asked.

I was still walking, and he was still driving beside me.

Tingles ran down my back. I kept walking, though a little faster.

"If you could come over to the car and look at this map, maybe you could help me," he said. "It won't take long. Just come over to the car and look at the map. I really need your help."

*Come over to the car? I don't think I'm supposed to go over to the car,* I thought.

He stopped his car and opened his door.

I ran. I ran as fast as I could. I didn't want him to follow me, so I ran behind the houses on the block. When I got to the end of the street, I had to cross Sackett to get to my street to go home. I was afraid to move from the backyard of the house where I was hiding. What if he saw me? What if he was waiting for me on Sackett Street? How was I going to get across the street?

I sat in that backyard for what felt like an hour but was probably much less. Finally, I ventured out. There was no one on the street. I ran all the way home.

I was late, of course, and my mom was furious. "Where have you been?" she snapped at me. "I was just about to call over there!"

"I'm sorry," I said, shaking and almost crying. "I, uh, stopped to look at some flowers in this lady's garden. I'm sorry."

"Go get ready for dinner," she said in her stern voice. "I'm extremely disappointed in you."

I didn't care. I was safe.

Maybe he was just a man in a car who needed directions. Maybe I was just a kid with an overactive imagination. Maybe I should have mentioned it to my mom. Maybe I could have ended up dead somewhere. Who knows? It could have been nothing, but I thought she should have noticed that something was wrong, that I was scared.

That's how kids think. We forget moms and dads are not mind readers. We don't know that we must speak out. At least, I didn't know it then. But we never talked about anything in my family anyway. What was one more thing?

# Seven

*When I was nine, Dad had an affair. It nearly killed Mom, and it* changed the direction of my life.

I remember waking up late at night to the sound of pots and pans banging around in the kitchen below my bedroom. Mom was yelling and throwing things. I ran into my sister's room across the hall and jumped into her bed. "What's happening?" I asked.

"Be quiet!" she said. We sat together and cried. I was terrified.

My parents separated for a while. I loved it when Dad was gone. Don't get me wrong—I missed him terribly, but our house was so peaceful without Dad and Mom snapping at each other all the time (or Mom snapping at Dad and Dad silently moping). When he was gone, there was no tension. Dad had moved into this cool little apartment, and I liked visiting him there. At home, Mom was much easier to be around. It was so quiet and nice; it seemed perfect to me.

One day, Dad told me about the affair. Back in the 1950s, new car showings were like Broadway openings. We'd all dress up in our best Sunday clothes and go to the dealership where Dad worked to see the shiny, fancy new Fords for that year. There were models there, standing by the cars and talking to people. One of them was tall, lean, and wearing a black, tight, full-length strapless gown. She looked like a movie star, like she'd stepped out of a magazine. On one of her breaks, Dad took me over to meet her. I'll call her "J." She was gracious and funny, and she and Dad laughed a lot as the three of us talked. She said she had a daughter about my age. I was in awe. I wanted to look like her, dress like her, be her.

Dad explained that the affair got started when J and her husband later returned to the dealership to purchase a car. "She 'accidentally' left her gloves behind, so I called her. We decided to meet for lunch the next day. That was how it all began. A few days later, we decided to meet at a motel for some private time."

I listened without saying anything.

"She was stunning," he said.

So was Mom, in her own way, I thought. There are pictures of my mother as a young woman laughing, flowers in her hair, with dimples that magically appeared when she smiled, and she had those spectacular legs. Dad took hundreds of pictures of her.

But J was "sophisticated, very stylish and modern, unlike anyone I had ever met," he said. "Her makeup and hair were perfect, and I could smell her perfume as we talked. She was soft-spoken and elegant." To a young girl, their affair sounded like a dramatic love story. "A few weeks later, her husband found out. He had followed J and me to the motel and called your mother," he said. "I caught hell when I got home." That was when the throwing of pots and pans began.

I felt terrible for Dad. I thought that my mother didn't really love my father. She wasn't nice to him, not as nice as this lady, or my dad wouldn't have wanted J. My dad was wonderful. This was my mother's fault. My mother never once discussed this with us; she never said a word. My dad's side of the story was the only one I ever heard, and it was just so dreamy, romantic, and heartbreaking.

If he was miserable with Mom and had met someone who made him happy, then why not get divorced? Why stay married if they were miserable? Then Mom could meet someone she loved, and everyone would be happy! It seemed so easy! Dad said he didn't want to lose his children (Mom wanted to take us back to St. Louis), plus he was Catholic, and Catholics didn't divorce. Evidently, it wasn't as easy as I thought. So eventually, he came home.

Mom kept a holy card in their bedroom that said, "When I forgive, I also forget." I believe she wanted to believe that.

I still believed my father's affair was all my mom's fault. I thought she didn't care about him enough, so she was to blame.

My sister saw things differently. To her, it was all my father's fault. He had done the unthinkable.

Dad and I were always together. I felt so special around him. We talked about the war and his time in the Army Air Force. We talked about his years growing up and how they'd had to move all the time during the Depression because they couldn't afford to pay rent. We talked about Nanny and Grandpa. Nanny had taken in boarders to supplement their income. I loved those stories about the "olden" days the best. We talked about books and politics and sports.

And we talked about sex.

One time, while Mom and Kathy were out shopping, Dad and I sat doing a puzzle on the dining room table. We'd been working silently for a while when I asked him, "Daddy, why did you have an affair?" It was pretty bold, but I felt like someone should tell me *something!*

He began confiding in me. He told me about his "disappointing honeymoon." He said, "Your Mom did not enjoy sex. You have something called a hymen. It's a thin piece of tissue covering your vagina. If you are a virgin, it will break during sex and sometimes leave a small amount of blood on the sheets. Mom was a virgin, and she said it hurt. I think it put her off sex for a while."

"Sex hurts?" I asked, a little scared.

"Just the first time. After that, it's smooth sailing."

"OK," I said, pretending I understood.

"Sometimes, there is such a strong attraction between a man and a woman that they just have to be together. It's like a magnet pulling them closer and closer until they slam into each other. That's what happened to me with J. It was pretty overwhelming. Sexual relations are a way to satisfy that urge. When a man and woman are enjoying sex, if they come to an orgasm at the same time, there is no better feeling on earth."

"What's an orgasm?" I asked.

"It's a pounding rush of … wait … Mom and Kathy are pulling into the driveway. We'll talk more later," he said as he headed to the door.

"What about love?" I called to him.

He stopped and turned to me. "Sex *is* love. It's the greatest form of love. No one will ever leave you if you are good at sex."

Those words planted a seed in the back of my brain that

lay dormant for years. I didn't even realize it was there. As the years passed, it would begin to grow like a silent form of cancer.

He was telling me this because he wanted me to be a better wife than Mom was. I also wanted to be a better wife than Mom. I never felt that the talks with my father were anything but a special connection. We didn't talk often. But when we did, if he shared the details of his sex life, it was only because he wanted me to be an enlightened, sexually aware young woman. On the other hand, he was very strict and did not encourage sexual activity before I was married. He was a lay minister at our church and wanted me to follow the rules of our faith. It was all a bit confusing. He didn't do anything to me—he never touched me. We just talked. "I wouldn't tell Mom or Kathy about our talks," he said. "They'd never understand. I love you," he said.

"I love you too, Daddy," I answered earnestly.

That's how it starts: quietly, innocently, secretly. Years later, I would read on LinkedIn that "covert abuse is subtle and veiled or disguised by actions that appear to be normal, at times loving and caring." I had no idea that what was happening was inappropriate. I was unaware that as these talks continued throughout my growing-up years, they would deeply affect my outlook on love and relationships.

For now, I looked forward to every moment with my dad, who gave the best hugs. I'd walk into the room, and he'd give me a huge bear hug. We'd just stand there, hugging each other, and I could feel my heart grow with love for him. I was safe.

# Eight

*My mother was truly a force of nature and way ahead of her time. She* was determined to make sure we got the education she thought we should have. When I was eleven, Mom took Kathy and me on a flight to New York, where we met our great-aunt, who worked at the United Nations. We took a tour and learned all about the UN and what it was doing to bring peace to the world and to improve relationships between countries. Mom felt it was important that we understand there were other people in the world who didn't have as good a life as we did and who had to fight to be heard. She wanted us to know that others lived without the freedom we took for granted.

After the UN we saw some of the historic sites of New York City. Then I finally saw my first Broadway show, *The King & I* with Yul Brynner. Wow! Now *that* was an introduction to Broadway! The singing, the dancing, the children, the costumes, the staging and lighting—it was beautiful and magical. It was a whole other world, and I was certain that someday I would be up there on the same stage. I was going to be an actress.

Mom also took us on many trips to St. Louis to visit Grandma Leona and our other relatives. Sometimes my father would come with us, and we'd pile into the station wagon to make the drive from Ohio. We'd flatten down the back seats and lay down blankets and pillows and bring along books and fun things to do on the long trip. We'd leave around 6:00 a.m. and travel until 5:00 p.m., stopping only for restroom breaks and lunch. When we got to Terre Haute, Indiana, we'd stay at a Holiday Inn, which was the best part of the trip. There was a pool where we could swim until bedtime. Early the next morning, we'd get back in the car for another four-hour trip. The speed limit was probably around fifty back then. In those days, no one bothered with seat belts.

Sometimes we flew, but most of the time Mom drove us herself. When it was just the three of us, my sister would sit up front with the map and help Mom navigate. With the whole back seat to myself, I could stretch out and get lost in my day-dreams. My sister and I would sing songs and see how many license plates we could identify from different states along the way. I looked at the clouds or at the houses we passed and won-dered what it would have been like to grow up on a farm or in a little brick home or a trailer. I tried to imagine who I would be if I had lived there instead of in my own home. Sometimes my sister and I would squabble and snap at each other, which drove Mom crazy. It was a long trip.

It was always fun to be with Mom's family. We had lots of cousins we rarely saw, and we got to play with them when we visited. Our distant relatives gave us lots of attention, and Mom was so happy to be back with what she called "*my* people."

I loved Grandma Leona. She was a nice woman, and she always made me feel like I was her favorite. But then, she made each of her grandchildren feel that way. That's why we all clustered around her. She was still a terrific baker and plied us with delicious treats.

Grandma Leona's duplex was in a row of brick houses that all looked alike. She shared a long backyard with the residents of the other unit in her duplex. There was an alley behind the building that we weren't supposed to play in, but we played there anyway. There was a staircase in the front of the house and a winding staircase in the back that led from the kitchen to the upstairs. It was hard to go up and down, and it terrified and fascinated me. It was always hot in Grandma's apartment. We kept a fan going all night when we visited, but it never helped. I must have gotten used to it because even now when it's sweltering hot, I'd rather have the windows open and a fan on than turn on the air-conditioning.

On one of our trips back to see the family, Mom had some errands to run with my aunt, and I went with her. I think I was about fourteen. I don't know where my sister was, but she probably had a job and wasn't able to come with us. At any rate, we stopped by Mom's brother's art studio. He was a successful painter who worked in both watercolor and oils, and the studio was so impressive. He and my mother and aunt decided it would be faster for the sisters to do their errands if they left me at the studio with him instead of taking me with them.

My uncle was soft-spoken and gentle. I adored him and was in awe of his talent. The studio walls were covered with his paintings, and the details of his work were breathtaking. I couldn't imagine doing what you loved and getting paid for it! He was always so kind, and though we didn't see him very often, we all loved being around him.

My mother and aunt had been gone only a few minutes when he invited me into his office. He had a chaise longue, which I thought was cool, and he asked me to have a seat. He sat down beside me. "I haven't seen you in a long time," he said. "You've grown."

"I have," I agreed.

"What are you going to do when you're done with school?" he asked.

"I want to be an actress!" I answered.

"I'm so proud of you. I know you'll do well. You've always had that special glow about you. You have that something that people will notice. You have talent, and you've grown into a beautiful young woman."

"Thanks," I said. "That means a lot to me."

"Do you know how pretty you are?" he asked.

"Trust me," I said, "no one ever calls me pretty. But it's nice of you to say so."

"Well, they should call you pretty, because you are," he said sweetly.

"Uh, thanks," I said, starting to feel a bit awkward.

"Why don't you lie down here and rest until your mom gets back?" he said. "You must be tired from your trip. You've barely gotten off the plane, and here you are. You haven't had a chance to relax at all."

"I'm not tired," I said.

"Come on, sweetie, lie down."

He was just being thoughtful, wasn't he? He had my best interests at heart, didn't he? So I lay down on the couch on my back.

"Are you comfortable?" he asked.

"Yeah, I guess," I replied.

He rose and closed the blinds on the window. "There, now you can sleep for a while," he said. Then he came back and lay down on his side next to me. My eyes were wide open. "Close your eyes, honey. Just rest," he said.

I closed my eyes. This was a little weird, but I mean, I used to sit on his lap as a little girl, and he would bounce me on his knee, so I shouldn't think anything of this, right?

"What a sweet girl you are. I have always loved you so," he said. "You were always my favorite." He brushed my hair from my face. My eyes popped open again.

"Close your eyes and just rest," he said.

OK, now it was getting really weird. He was stroking my hair gently.

"Sleep," he said. Then, very slowly, he brought his hand across my body to my other shoulder and gently slid it down my arm. "Your skin is so soft," he said as he began stroking my arm. This continued for a few minutes before his hand touched my breast, and like a rocket, I jumped off the couch.

"I'm really not tired after all," I said. I dashed into the outer room and began looking at all the beautiful pictures. He stayed in his office and closed the door.

I knew from my talks with my dad that men had their needs, but this was terrifying to me. I was out there for a long time, alone, looking at those paintings, his easels, his color palettes and paintbrushes. I tried to lose myself in the light and detail in each painting with such intensity that it gave me a headache, but I wasn't about to take my eyes off them. I thought that if I just kept looking at them, I'd be safe.

Finally, my mom came back. "Did you enjoy yourself?" she asked.

"Sure," I answered. How could I tell her? She would be crushed.

Then my uncle came out, and we all exchanged hugs and said, "I love you." And that was that.

Whenever he'd call the house after that day, my mother would put first my sister and then me on the phone to say hello to him, and I'd get physically ill trying to talk to him about friends and school. Listening to his sleazy voice was painful for me. Yet I could not tell my mother what had happened. It would have been horrible of me to do that to her. She loved him so much. And nothing had really happened, had it? So it was no big deal.

When he passed away years later, each of us received some of his paintings. I had my husband take the ones that were given to me and toss them in the garbage can.

That incident, that "nothing" that had happened, would play over and over in my head for years.

# Nine

*It was 1965, and I was going for my first job interview. I was sixteen* and had just gotten my driver's license. I had heard from a friend that a local discount store was hiring clerks, but Mom and Dad wanted me to keep babysitting. What kind of job was that for a girl in high school? All my friends already had jobs for the summer, so I was way behind.

I took a long time to get ready. I had thick hair, and I washed it and set it in big pink and green rollers that made my curly hair straighter. Then I spent an hour under the hair dryer with a pink bonnet that puffed out when you turned on the machine. You had to be careful that the rubber hose didn't burn your arm while you sat there. But it was always a good opportunity to read *Teen* magazine and see what was happening with the Beatles and all the other stars who lived such fabulous lives. After my hair was dry, I'd get my rat-tailed comb, and after a little teasing on top (not too much, or Mom would flip), I'd be almost ready. I didn't wear face makeup (Dad would flip on that one), but I could use lip gloss and mascara. Dad wasn't too happy about the mascara, but Mom was on my side.

I really wanted the job. It was only five minutes from my house, and it was at a large discount store where anyone could buy almost anything at bargain prices. I was hoping to be a checkout girl.

The lady at the service desk instructed me to go to the office at the rear of the store. There, a man of about forty who wore a shirt, tie, and dress pants met me and showed me into his office. I sat in a chair in front of his desk, and he asked me several questions while reading the form I had filled out. We talked for a while, and then he asked if I'd step into a side office. There, on another desk, were several large blue books containing what he explained were computer printouts of everything in the store. He opened one of the books and asked me to look through it. "Stand right here," he said.

"I don't understand," I replied. "You want me to look through these pages?"

"Yes," he said, stepping behind me. "I want you to familiarize yourself with our inventory. It's important that you have knowledge of our stock if you are to work here. Just stay there and don't turn around."

I stayed there, standing, as I looked at the pages. It seemed so odd. Was this a normal part of a job interview? I looked at a page and turned it, then another and another and another.

"Don't turn around," he said. He sounded nervous.

I kept looking at the printouts. I was getting a shivery feeling up my spine. Something wasn't right. Why was I looking at these stupid pages? How was this going to help me be a cashier or a salesclerk? Did everyone have to know the entire inventory of the store before they could work here? Why didn't he want me to turn around?

It seemed like I stood there for a very long time, turning pages, while he stood several feet behind me in this area not much bigger than a closet. After a while, the room went very still. I took a chance and turned around. He was gone. I was completely alone and totally uncertain as to what I was supposed to do.

A few moments later, he came back into the room, led me back into his office, and told me to sit in the chair. "I think you'll do well here," he said. "You've got the job and you can start on Monday."

"Thank you," I said. And I left.

I drove home totally confused. What the heck had that been all about? What had gone on in that room? Was this one of those "men have needs" things? I ran into the house and told my father. I knew my father could explain it. He knew everything. He could handle every situation. He could fix anything. He was the greatest man in the universe. Surely, he would fix this, and I would get my job, and everything would be all right.

After I told him, my dad got into his car and drove off to the store. When he came back, I asked him what had happened.

"You aren't working there," he said. "Now go to bed." And that was the end of it.

I knew a lot about sex for my age, but nothing about predatory male behavior and my rights as a young woman to stand up for myself. If I had, I might have saved myself a lot of heartache in my later life. I had walked into that store unsuspecting. I had walked out not that much smarter. Back then no one told me that I was a strong and valuable young woman who had a voice I could use whenever I felt some man was not treating me with the respect I deserved. So I continued along in my foggy, confused, Pollyanna life, thinking the best of everyone. I knew things, but I didn't really understand them, and I certainly didn't know that I had the power to change anything.

I simply tucked this event away with the other movies in my mind of the things that had happened to me, wondering what it was about me that drew in the creepy people.

# Ten

*Dad was very strict about our education. My sister and I had to go to* all-girls schools, and there was no arguing about it. Dad was hard on Kathy: she had to travel by bus an hour to and from her school and never got to take part in after-school activities or date very much. I didn't want that to happen to me. I wanted a social life. I fought to attend a school nearby that had an affiliation with an all-boys school. They functioned as our football team, and we took part in each other's plays. We had two homecoming dances and two proms. It was great. My sister spent a lot of time away from home but got a terrific education. I stayed closer and had more fun. I got my way. I always got my way.

Students weren't allowed to be in clubs during freshman year, so the summer before our sophomore year, my friends and I mulled over how we would audition for the Drama Club. I came up with the idea of doing a scene from *The Wizard of Oz*. I gathered together seven of my friends, and we memorized all the lines from the moment the Wizard bellows to Dorothy, "Why have you come back?" and Dorothy says, "If you please, sir, we brought you the broomstick of the Wicked Witch of the West." The Wizard had the biggest part in the scene, but I didn't care. I was playing Dorothy.

Our audition took nine and a half minutes. The Drama Club gave us the extra time since there were eight of us doing the scene. When we finally got to "There's no place like home!" the room erupted in cheers.

The teacher said, "Wow! Who put that together?"

"Marylee!" said my friends.

"That was the most impressive audition I've ever seen. I'm not even going to wait for you to check the list tomorrow. You're all in!"

We jumped up and down, screaming. You'd have thought we won an Oscar! Obviously, I was meant for the theater.

I took part in many of our high school plays at both the girls' and boys' schools. The boys' school was run by the Brothers of the Holy Cross. The difference between priests and brothers, though both are ordained, is that the brothers take additional vows of poverty, charity, and obedience. Priests can make money and buy boats, houses, and fancy cars. Brothers cannot. Our school was run by the Holy Humility of Mary Catholic Nuns. They were deeply religious, often stern, and sometimes funny, and they always kept to themselves.

I auditioned for and was cast as Elmire in *Tartuffe* as well as Guinevere in *A Connecticut Yankee in King Arthur's Court* at the boys' school. There I learned about acting and diving into the thoughts, skin, and inner workings of a character. I loved being someone else.

I remember an experience from our rehearsal for *A Connecticut Yankee in King Arthur's Court*. We had just been given our costumes to wear for dress rehearsal. My dress was stunning—brocaded, long, and elegant with billowy sleeves. But that hat! The costume makers had designed cones with scarves falling from the pointed tops for most of the girls to wear. Mine looked slightly more like a crown but had a shower curtain veil attached all around it. With my hair pulled off my face, I looked awful. I looked like a boy. The second female lead in the cast looked beautiful. Her pretty face, soft features, ski-jump nose, and big eyes were made even more outstanding by that ridiculous hat. My angular, Gaelic features were harsh and unappealing. I was so disappointed. I mentioned this to our director, Brother Jerome, and he said, "Yes, but *you* have talent." Wait, what? I think that was supposed to be a compliment, but it felt like a confirmation.

I also remember an enlightening conversation that occurred during a rehearsal for *Tartuffe*. I told Brother Jerome that I had a crush on a boy named Thom who was in the cast. Brother Jerome looked at me and said, "I'm sorry, honey, but I think he likes boys." What did that mean? How could a boy like a boy? He proceeded to explain it to me. Wow, I had not expected that. That was something my dad had never told me about.

There were also showcase musical productions each year at the boys' school and talent shows galore at both the girls' and boys' schools. The combined schools created a yearly musical production that they called *Showcase!* My friend Tom and I were selected by the director to sing "People Will Say We're In Love" from *Oklahoma*. His eyelashes were long and thick. I wondered why boys were so lucky, while girls had to pack on mascara. The best part of the show was when I got to dance all alone with the football team while they sang "Hello, Dolly!"

from, of course, the musical *Hello, Dolly!* The guys, dressed in tuxedos and top hats, were quite a sight considering their usual football ruggedness, and the girls in the audience went wild. The boys sang and did a kick-line, and the audience cheered. As they began singing the second chorus, I came out as Dolly in a long, flowing green chiffon gown and danced with them. Oh, the whistles and cheers that got! When they picked me up at the end and lifted me into the air, I threw my arms up for a showstopping finale. That number caught the eye of a schoolmate's brother. I began dating this handsome, tall, blue-eyed guy who was a year older than I and attending college. We were in for a summer of fun. At eighteen, emotions are so *big*, and I went bonkers for this sweet guy.

Meanwhile, I still had to graduate before the summer began. At the girls' school, I was part of a handpicked singing group called the Marionettes. There were eight of us, and we sang at assemblies and special events; it was a big honor to be in that group. Those days were fun and happy. Offstage, I wasn't particularly popular, but onstage, I felt like someone special. Onstage, I was safe. Onstage, I could do anything, be anyone. Anything connected with singing, dancing, and theater was a happy, warm, safe place for me, and I never wanted to leave that world.

It had always been the theater that held the most happiness for me, so when it came time to enter college, I wanted to major in theater.

"Absolutely not," Dad said. "Do you know how many people fail in that field? You'll never get a job. It's a dream."

So since I'd been on the high school paper, I decided to major in journalism instead. I'm pretty sure that if you want to do something, you really should study *that* something and not something else. Otherwise, you end up being good at some-thing you like but for which you have no passion.

The summer before college, a group of us who'd been doing plays in high school decided we were really going to break out and do some serious drama. We were *actors* (seriously minded and into our craft, not just playing), and we were going to step away from the protective shell of the all-boy/all-girl schools and dive into real theater. We talked the Weathervane Playhouse in Akron into letting us use their annex to produce some plays. The boys chose *American Buffalo* by David Mamet, about three guys who conspire to steal a coin collection from a wealthy man. Much more happens in the play, but I'm not sure if the guys chose it as their breakout piece because of the overall play or because there are so many swear words thrown back and forth onstage. We were avant-garde in our approach, true actors, deep into our craft, finding depth and meaning in our work.

The next play was *Lysistrata* by Aristophanes. I was cast in the title role. Lysistrata was a fascinating woman who met with all the women of Greece whose husbands were fighting the Peloponnesian War. She asked them to withhold sex until their husbands agreed to sign a peace treaty to end the war. Don't you just love this idea? Do you think it would work today? My mom and dad came to see the show, and during my big speech, when I asked the women to promise to refuse to have sex with their husbands, my father, in his most disapproving tone, said loudly, "Marylee!"

I was still dating my friend's brother. All summer, he'd drive his little blue MG to my house, and we'd go for long walks together, take long rides in his cute little car with the top down, or just talk. We held hands, and there was an occasional kiss. It was all so innocent. I was crazy about him, but at the end of the summer, he broke up with me. I was devastated and wanted to know why, but my father saw me crying as we sat on the porch of my house talking, and he kicked the boy out, telling him that he could never come back, call me, or talk to me again. I was furious.

"I want to talk to him!" I yelled at my dad. "I want to know what happened. I love him, and you don't have the right to stop me from getting answers!"

Much to my father's credit, he got on the phone with the young man, apologized, and told him to come back. He did return and told me he'd been dating another girl for a long time before we began dating. She had gone away for the summer, and he had wanted to go out with me. He cared for me, even loved me, but he loved her more. Now that she was back, he had to end it. This hurt, but it made sense. It wasn't the answer I wanted, but it was an answer I could live with. It must have been hard for my dad to make that call.

# $\mathscr{E}leven$

*In September 1967 I entered Kent State University to study journal-*ism. I loved writing, and I seemed to be pretty good at it. But I had more fun when I pledged the sorority Chi Omega. I managed to get through the initiation intact. We pledges were asked to pull a stunt that our already-initiated sisters wouldn't know about, so I arranged for all the pledges to flee to my house for one night. The next morning, Mom and Dad came downstairs to find sleeping beauties all over the living room and dining room floors. Being good sports about it, Mom made coffee for all of us, while Dad got doughnuts for everyone, and a successful pledge stunt was completed.

Mom wasn't always unhappy. It seemed that when she was out of the house, she came alive. She belonged to a charity group, volunteered at the hospital, played cards in a bridge club, was a member of the women's group at church, golfed, and enjoyed throwing parties. For the parties, she would get out the silver, china, and crystal and put on a stunning dress to entertain lots of her and Dad's friends. My sister and I loved seeing them have fun for a change, often peeking around the stairs to watch them.

I'm sure Mom thought that being part of a sorority would be a wonderful social experience for her daughter. But I never got to "go active" with Chi Omega, which would have meant attending the ceremony where I would have been made a full member. Instead, I pledged myself to a group committed to changing the world.

The musical touring company Up with People (UWP) was coming to our town. There were a lot of protests during the sixties about the war, racism, and equal rights. Up with People took the passion of our generation and turned it into a musical demonstration that would sing out about these issues in a positive way. According to J. Blanton Belk, the head of the company, Up with People had a "perilous, exacting, demanding mission in history," and though it didn't promise anything, it hoped to raise up new youth leadership from countries around the world through music, song, and interaction of world cultures.

I'd seen Up with People on TV and begged to go see the live show. Mom and Dad took me, and I was struck by the universality of their theme song: "Up, up with people! / You meet them wherever you go / Up, up with people! / They're the best kind of folks we know / If more people were for people / All people everywhere / There'd be a lot less people to worry about / And a lot more people who care."

After the show, I talked with some of the cast members about what they were doing for our generation, what it was like being a part of the troupe, and where they were going next.

It turned out they were having interviews the next day for new casting, and I went, along with my cousin Denise. Denise remembers going into a room with a piano while I sat outside talking with one of the cast members, then vice versa. I don't remember singing, but I vividly remember the interview. We talked about me as a person, the shows I had done, my thoughts and my feelings about our generation, and what I hoped I could contribute to creating a better world. I told my interviewer about visiting my aunt at the United Nations and how Mom had wanted us to understand the different cultures and beliefs that made up the world.

The company invited us both to come with them, but Denise's mom said, "No, you are going to college." I was determined to go, however, and just like that, I knew my life was going to change.

Mom and Dad went to the show with me the next night. They talked to the directors to be assured of my safety and that I'd be able to go to church every Sunday.

I went home and packed my bag. I told my parents, "If I don't go, I'll regret it for the rest of my life." I was leaving my ordinary black-and-white world and heading for Technicolor to do something important. It was meant to be.

Leaving college after one semester meant nothing to me. I wasn't supposed to be a newspaper reporter; I was supposed to be an actress. I was supposed to see the world and do something amazing with my life. This was my chance.

The next morning, I said goodbye to Mom and Dad at the local Newman Center, a Catholic youth organization in Akron. My friend's brother miraculously showed up to say goodbye. He was a member of the Newman Center, so he may have just been there, or perhaps he had found out about my plans and knew I was leaving. At any rate, I was so glad to see him. He even gave me a kiss goodbye, which caused some commotion on the bus, and wished me luck. I was as happy as I'd ever been. I was going on a great adventure. I stepped onto the tour bus and never looked back. Little did I suspect the roads I would travel and the effect they would have on my future.

I was unaware, as I joined the group, that Up with People was a function of a group called Moral ReArmament (MRA), a religious sect. The musical group had been created in 1965 at an MRA conference held on Mackinac Island in Michigan. I not only had been cast in a musical but also had become part of this moral movement. No one had bothered to mention that part. When I did learn, I wasn't quite sure how I felt about it or what it meant, but I'd later learn how deep, narrow, and restrictive its code was. At that time, I just wanted to leave home and see the world!

We headed south, making stops for performances along the way, through Kentucky, Tennessee, and Alabama, with our final stop being Texas. My voice was finally categorized: lyric soprano. However, I had to learn the entire show before I could go onstage, so at the start of the trip, I was placed at the soundboard, where I could listen to the songs as we went. By the time we got to Texas, I had become part of the cast and was having a ball. I don't remember in what city I first stepped onstage, but I remember feeling exuberant, alive, and part of something bigger than myself.

There were four buses carrying the cast: an all-girls bus, an all-boys bus, the songwriting bus, and the high school bus where kids sixteen and older studied as we traveled. It didn't take me long to figure out that the songwriters' bus was coed. I'm not stupid: I started writing songs.

Riding on the bus at night after a show and on our way to a new town was magical. The bus would be dark except for a flashlight here or there from people reading. A few hushed voices could be heard in quiet conversation, but most of the cast were resting. Then, from the very back of the bus, someone would pick up a harmonica and lull us all to sleep.

Because of my strong voice, I was moved up from the back row and placed in one of the small groups around the microphones. But I knew it wouldn't be long before I was up out front as a soloist. I was certain of it. It was my destiny.

We stayed in people's homes in each town we went to, and I ended up rooming with one of the group's lead soloists. She taught me about the practice of writing in a guidance book. Each morning, during quiet time, we were supposed to write down our thoughts and try to get guidance from God in preparing for the day.

One Saturday morning, we left our hosts' home because my roommate had to attend a special meeting. We were dropped off at a church, where she said, "I won't be long," and went inside without me. It was a blazing-hot day, and I was supposed to wait outside until the meeting was over. I tried to find a cool place to sit for what turned out to be an hour and a half without anything to do. There were no cell phones back then, so I couldn't write messages or play games to pass the time. I was bored out of my mind and getting angry. When she finally returned, I blasted her. "What were you doing all this time? What was so secretive that I couldn't come inside? How could you leave me sitting here like that? What the heck kind of group did I get myself into?"

She apologized and said they had just been discussing the upcoming tour and talking about some of the cast members who needed extra intervention. "I'm sorry. You could have come in. It wasn't that secret. Just some of the leaders trying to organize the group."

"Don't let it happen again!" I snapped. Years later, I would be part of the leadership group and responsible for indoctrinating new members. I never left anyone alone to bake in the sun while I fulfilled my responsibilities.

To me, being part of MRA came to mean traveling, doing our show with purpose, and living by high moral standards. I jumped in with both feet. We were, after all, on a glorious mission. Imagine being given the chance to change the world!

Finally, we hit Texas for Christmas. We spent a week in leaky tents in Leakey (pronounced LAY-key), Texas, while it poured down rain. The land was part of an MRA member's estate, and though we suffered through the rain and had to trudge through mud to get to the food tent, we had a great time, singing, laughing, and constantly feeling reinforced about our mission.

As we headed back to the East Coast, cast members came and went, and when one of our soloists left, I was given my first song. I was never afraid, never nervous. I was well-rehearsed and prepared. I was doing what I was meant to do. Those solos were my moments to shine.

We performed at Fort Benning, a US Army post straddling the Alabama–Georgia border where more than 120,000 military members and their families resided. This show was a phenomenal success. How could it not be? We were singing about peace for the world, and they were providing it for us.

I stayed with the wealthiest and the poorest of families as we traveled around the country, including stays in governors' mansions and poor homes where mice scurried around during the night. I met some of the country's best people and some of its worst, those whose hardened hearts still divide us and keep us from remembering that underneath it all, when you peel back that top layer of skin, we are all exactly alike.

We were in Asheville, North Carolina, rehearsing, when Mr. Belk came to see us. It was always exciting when he was around. He gathered us together and talked about our mission in life and the opportunity we had to make the world better. And then he surprised us by bellowing, "You're all going to Italy!" The screams and cheers were deafening. We began to learn some Italian and to translate some of our songs.

Most of us had never been out of the country before; this would be my first trip abroad. I was crazy with excitement. I packed everything I owned into one huge bag, even though I knew that whatever I took, I also had to carry. I didn't care. If those little wheelie things lasted, I would pull the load anywhere. But who knew that there would be so many steps in Italy?

My mother and father came to the airport to see us off. Mom was nervous and misty-eyed. She had always wanted to travel to Europe, Africa, or anywhere overseas but had never gotten the chance. Dad was sort of happy, sort of sad. His little girl was leaving home, and he didn't quite know how he felt about it. He was sure I was going to get into some sort of horrible trouble, and yet he was proud that I was fearless in doing this. As for me, I was going to live life and see Italy! I couldn't wait to leave. A hug here, a kiss there, and I ran toward the plane. At last, I was going to see what life abroad was all about!

We landed in Milan, where we would perform our first show. Culture shock! My tiny-town toes touched the ground, and I was in another dimension. Suddenly, everything had a history that dated to long before anything in my young country. This struck me as we looked out of the windows of the bus that took us to our hotel. The buildings, the vivid colors of the houses, and the materials used to construct them—the entire landscape—created the first of many mental photos I've kept in my mind. I kept sending postcards home so that my parents could get a glimpse of this fascinating country and its rich culture.

It's not that there wasn't the occasional unwelcome surprise. At the youth hostel where we checked in, I soon encountered something I could have happily lived without experiencing. I learned how to take a shower in cold water. Jumping in and out to get clean was fine, but washing my hair was absolute torture. It made me think of how some people lived without hot running water their whole lives.

Our setup team had arrived in advance to build the stage in an ornately carved and gilded old theater. The rest of us went to a reception in a government building, where officials welcomed us with an array of delicacies to sample. I tasted my first caviar and thought it was horrible! I have since changed my mind.

After that, a large group of us went off into the streets, singing and handing out flyers for the show. Others in the group, who spoke Italian, were dispersed to businesses, schools, and radio programs to help drum up an audience.

We opened the show with "Fratelli d'Italia," the national theme song, and the crowd went *kraze!* We sang our theme song, "Up with People," in Italian, and in the middle of the show, there was a medley of songs from around the world sung in their original languages. It was a night of stirring emotions and huge applause.

Soon, we began our tour of Italy by hopping on a bus and heading out into the countryside.

Our first stop after Milan was Venice. I was fascinated by its canals, gondolas, and bridges. No cars! We went to see all the pigeons at the Piazza San Marco. If you held your arm out straight, a pigeon would land on it! Who knew? That didn't happen at home. Many years later, my son would take a high school trip to Venice and feed pigeons in the same spot, as would my daughter and her family years after that. Recently, I went there with my husband and reenacted my pigeon experience. Little did I know as an eighteen-year-old girl standing in the piazza that my future family would one day be standing in the same spot.

The place I was most looking forward to was Rome. Because I was from a devoutly Catholic family, it held an extreme reverence for me. The pope was there since Rome was the seat of the Holy Roman Church. I could hardly contain my excitement.

We had to walk a lot of places. The bus dropped us off, and then we hiked around the streets of Rome. One of the cast members, who had gone on in advance to help set up our tour, led the way and interpreted for us when necessary. I wasn't really listening to what he said because I was more fascinated by the guy himself. He was so alive, so full of energy, and so handsome. He was one of the many bilingual members of the cast, in his case fluent in English and Spanish. He told us picking up Italian had been easy for him since there was an 80 percent similarity between the two languages. It was impressive to me.

Rome was full of history, and I was standing in the middle of it! We were walking down an old cobblestone street when I saw some huge pillars ahead. As I circled one of them, I turned to one of my friends and said, "Wow, this must have been part of something incredible once." As I turned back around, I stepped into St. Peter's Square. There it was, in all its splendor: the Papal Palace, the Sistine Chapel, and St. Peter's Basilica. I looked around at the courtyard with its fountains, birds flying around, and people everywhere. I felt as though we'd walked right into a dream. There were a few vendors, and we browsed to see what they were selling. I stopped to purchase rosaries, "blessed by the pope," for my mother and father, who still said the rosary every night. I knew they would love them and hold them dear.

We went to the Sistine Chapel first. Some five hundred years after these works of art were painted, tourists still flock to see them. The most stunning was Michelangelo's fresco *The Last Judgment* and the famous painting *The Creation of Adam* on the ceiling of the Sistine Chapel. In the painting, God reaches out to touch Adam's finger and give him life. The arc of the ceiling, the colors, the height, the beauty, the skill, the minute detail, and the difficulty of painting it took my breath away! My neck began to hurt from looking up at it for so long, and I was getting worried about making it to St. Peter's Basilica in time to see the pope, who was to appear that very afternoon. He would be carried on his platform chair down the central aisle, past all the visitors.

There were hundreds of people there just for a glimpse of Pope John Paul II. I remember watching TV when he was elected, waiting for a white puff of smoke to emerge from the Sistine Chapel signaling his election. My family's devotion to the church and this new pope was all-consuming. Getting to actually see him would mean so much to them and, of course, to me. We had to make sure our arms and heads were covered to be respectful of the sacred significance of his position and that of the Roman Catholic Church.

The cathedral was huge, with many chapels and beautiful statues, and we stopped for a long look at Michelangelo's famous *Pieta*. We worked our way into the main area where the pope, beloved by all the faithful, head of the Holy Roman Catholic Church, and respected by millions, would bless us. We would see him! I was surely in heaven.

It was a mass of people, but a few of us squeezed as close to the front as we could without offending anyone. When it was time for the pope to begin his trip down the aisle, the entire church erupted in chants of "Papa! Papa!" Clapping and cheering in church! I couldn't believe it. My mother would be aghast! We weren't even allowed to whisper in church. As children, we had to sit with our hands folded neatly and our ankles crossed and never, ever talk or risk the wrath of our mother. We stood or knelt, and we prayed with our hands in the appropriate position. We answered the prayers in Latin until the Mass was changed to English, but that was it. If we tried to talk, we'd get a strict glance from Mom and later a stern lecture followed by Hail Marys. So I was astounded by the atmosphere here!

We found ourselves shoulder to shoulder with strangers who'd come together in this brotherhood of humanity's faith in God and in awe of our opportunity to see a man of God who would one day be a part of history. The pope had begun his trip down the aisle. Excitement was mounting. We were crammed and jammed, but I could feel the halo forming above my head. The crowd was yelling and pushing, and I was a sardine in a tin can of Christ our Lord. Then there he was! The pope! He was getting closer and closer. I could sense his presence even though I couldn't yet see him.

Just then, I felt a hand move up the side of my leg, slowly pushing up my skirt. Higher and higher it went, sliding toward my underwear. I was trapped. I couldn't move. There were too many people. The pope was nearly in front of me, but I couldn't focus on him. My mind was focused on the hand. I screamed at the man to get away, but he didn't stop. I tried to push at his hand, but my arms were stuck. I tried to yell to my friends, "There's a man behind me—get him off!" but they couldn't hear me. The noise in the cathedral was too loud.

Then, as the pope was about to pass right in front of me, the man slid his hand to the top of my underpants and pushed his body up against me. There was no mistaking it: that hard, undeniable feeling of a man's penis, erect and full, solid as a rock, forced against my lower back. I was eighteen years old and a virgin. I'd had no sexual experience whatsoever, but I knew what was happening to me. There I was, trying to see the pope, and a man was molesting me! I was yelling to everyone around me, "Get him off me!" but they couldn't hear, or they didn't understand. They were caught up in the excitement, the glory of seeing the pope, while I fought against a hand and a hard-on.

I struggled with all the force in my being to keep him from going any further and finally pushed away from him and through the crowd. By the time I got to a place where I felt safe, and I turned back, the pope was no longer visible. The only opportunity I would have for this precious moment was gone. He had passed by, and I had missed him. My moment in history was ruined.

We went on to do our show in Rome, but the fantasy I had created about Rome, all that it meant, all that I had wanted it to be, had been dulled by this experience. I never told anyone about it. Why bother? It was over. I couldn't wait to leave town.

Of all the places in the world where this could have happened, it's hard to imagine that I would have been an unsuspecting child in St. Peter's Basilica. I added it to the list of movies in my mind and went on.

# *Twelve*

*After a performance in Rome in another historic gilded theater, we piled* on the bus for a quick trip to the Catacombs of St. Callixtus. Beneath the ground, nearly half a million Christians were entombed, including many martyrs and sixteen popes. We were looking around, mesmerized by the magnitude of what we were seeing, when someone came to tell us that Robert Kennedy had been assassinated. We didn't believe him. President John Kennedy had been assassinated in 1963. What was he talking about? Robert Kennedy was running for president, and he was the hope of our young generation; he couldn't have been killed. Our guide took us outside, and we gathered around and learned the truth. I had been fourteen when John Kennedy was shot. I had seen through my parents' eyes how devastated they were. Now I was eighteen years old. Too young to vote (you had to

be twenty-one back then), I was still part of an extremely polit-
ical time and was keenly aware of Robert Kennedy's campaign
to win the White House.

Now Bobby was dead. John had belonged to my parents,
but Bobby was ours. It struck the hearts of so many in our
group who had held out hope for the future.

In the constant rush that was our schedule, we got back
on the bus, stopped quickly at the Trevi Fountain to throw in
some coins so we could return one day, and headed south to,
among other places, Naples.

Often prior to the entire company's arrival in a town, we
would send out an advance team of a few soloists and some
members of the band to sing on a truck or trailer bed or in
the streets or schools, to drum up publicity for our upcoming
show. I went with a small group to Naples. We'd done all our
exhausting dashing around and handing out of flyers and singing when we decided we needed pizza. Not the fat, thick, red
sauce–soaked pizza I knew, but a thin, cheesy, delicious pizza!
We parked our van filled with instruments and suitcases and
went into the restaurant. When we came out, the van was gone,
along with our instruments and everything we had brought
to Europe with us. The police came and took a report while
we waited to be rescued by the rest of the cast. I couldn't have
cared less about my clothes, but my old boyfriend, my friend's
brother, had sent me a touching letter saying how proud of me
he was for doing something so important. He wrote that he
treasured the time we'd spent together and ended by quoting
Donovan's song "Catch the Wind": "Ah, but I might as well
try and catch the wind." He was saying goodbye. I had also
lost my camera and my pictures and things I had purchased,

but I was most upset about that letter. I grieved the loss of that letter. Our families wired us money to replace our lost goods, and we returned the clothes we'd borrowed from our friends, but the letter was irreplaceable.

# $\mathcal{T}$hirteen

*In 1969 we went to France, Spain, and Germany, and I truly believed* that life couldn't get any better. In France we saw the Eiffel Tower and passed the Arc de Triomphe. We passed but did not go into the Louvre and Notre-Dame de Paris. I am so happy that I got to see Notre-Dame in its full glory. On April 15, 2019, it suffered a devastating fire from which it may never recover. Though I believe that the French people loved our show, they were more conservative and quieter than the excited Italians. We sped up the pace of the show a bit for the quick and polite applause.

While in France, we received an invitation to perform for the Belgian royalty, King Baudouin and Queen Fabiola, at their Royal Arboretum in Laeken. You may not have heard of them. Baudouin suffered miserably as a child with the untimely death of his grandfather, King Albert I of Belgium, as well as the death of his mother, Queen Astrid. During his growing-up years, he had to contend with bombings, accusations of treason against the family, and exile. His father, Leopold III, was unpopular and forced to abdicate. Baudouin became king at the age of twenty-one. Fabiola, born in Madrid, had an ideal childhood, came from an aristocratic family, and lived in a castle. How did they meet? An Irish nun became a matchmaker and found Fabiola to be an ideal match for the king. They fell in love through their common religious beliefs and faith.

The royal couple's arboretum, where we would perform, was enormous, allowing birds to fly freely among the plants, shrubbery, and trees. Our team arranged risers in the garden where the king and queen were seated with other guests. The show always began with our running onto the stage from all directions while beginning to sing. It was fun to see them laugh with enthusiasm. After the show, we presented flowers to Queen Fabiola. She was wearing a simple white dress, and he was wearing a suit. They were unassuming and gracious and spoke to us about our ideals and our commitment to making a better world.

Spain was next. I stayed with a marvelous family in Madrid. Their flat was on the second floor of a charming old three-story building. They had two sons, about eighteen and twenty, and after a wonderful dinner, the boys disappeared while I talked with their mother and father using my broken Spanish. Soon we heard music, and my hosts led me to the veranda and opened the doors. I looked down over the iron railing, and in the courtyard below stood the boys with some of their friends, guitars in hand, playing and singing! I could hardly believe it. Here I was, now nineteen years old, standing under a beautiful star-filled sky on a veranda in Spain, being serenaded by a group of young Spanish men. How incredibly romantic was that? It was right out of a novel.

When we were in Valencia, we got to perform at the Plaza de Toros, a bullring. Thousands and thousands of people crammed into the bullring. It was the most surreal feeling to step out for my solo in front of so many people. To have that huge place packed with people, both on the floor in chairs and standing shoulder to shoulder in the stands that circled the bullring, was a thrill of a lifetime. The Spanish people are the most lively and vibrant people in the world. When we finished with our songs, they would stand on their seats, waving handkerchiefs, applauding, cheering, and just going wild and crazy. I'd never felt anything like it, nor would I again.

We also performed in Toledo, Seville, and Barcelona. I've forgotten more than I remember, so the order of the trip and some of the cities are a little hazy. But then, I was always a little hazy. I was living this incredible life, but at the same time I was lost in the things going on in my head.

Traveling by bus and train in Europe was exhausting, so they sent some of the soloists to a cabin in Geneva, Switzerland, to rest while the rest of the cast took a train to Germany. The directors were depending on our voices, and it was important that we be able to sing without sounding like we hadn't slept in weeks, which we hadn't. Those of us who got to go to Geneva slept and rested and walked. We had no water for a while because the pipes in our chalet were frozen, but we had an amazing time in another new country with a group of warm, hospitable, and generous people. I remember taking a hike with one of the other soloists and sitting on a huge rock, looking at the Alps, so tall and majestic, covered in snow and sparkling, as the sun warmed us. "Toto," I said, "I don't think we're in Kansas anymore."

Germany was everything you see in pictures. It was full of enchanting chalets and beckoning pubs we couldn't go into, though I brought back some awesome German beer steins. I took my first trip on a cable car to the top of a mountain. There was also the ugly wall looming over much of the city of Berlin.

The latter sight stayed with me for a long time. I was consistently reminded that freedom is precious and must be fought for. Long after I left, on June 12, 1987, President Ronald Reagan gave his famous "tear down this wall" speech in West Berlin. The Berlin Wall was finally destroyed on November 9, 1989, and I shed tears of joy.

We had done our part in Europe to demonstrate the importance of unity with songs like "Freedom Isn't Free" ("Freedom isn't free / You've got to pay a price / You've got to sacrifice / For your liberty"). I was proud to be part of those asking our generation to unite and work toward peace.

# Fourteen

*Back in the United States, we learned that we were going to be doing* a TV special. I couldn't wait for my friends and family to see us on television. The show was on NBC, introduced by Bob Hope and sponsored by Coca-Cola. Being in that huge studio, with all its cameras and lights, was a dream come true! There was a camera that pulled in for close-ups, a camera for the long shot of the group, and a camera that started at one end and panned the length of the risers to get each of us as we sang. I got a lot of letters from my family, friends, and relatives who were thrilled to see me on TV. I never saw the production myself, but I have some great pictures of us performing in the studio.

We headed south again for Christmas, this time to Santa Fe, New Mexico. One of the songs I cowrote, "New Dimension," was added to the show, and it was thrilling to have the entire cast perform it. ("We're launching into a new dimension, yeah

/ You can come along if you want to / It's a brand new world that we're gonna see / We're launching into a new dimension, yeah.")

But it wasn't all fun. There were some hard times on the road. We stayed in homes, and not everyone was always welcoming. Like I said, there was a dark side to America that still exists. We do it to ourselves. We have the power to change it, but change is difficult when people hold hatred in their hearts.

We were in Arkansas in a little town that I will not name, and I was helping do setup. When you set up for the cast to come in, that meant you handled the publicity, got homes arranged for the cast and crew to stay in, made appearance arrangements, and got all other necessary pre-show work done prior to the arrival of the cast and crew. We went to a radio station to talk about an interview we were going to do the next day and what we wanted to accomplish. We told the DJ that we were going to ask people to open their homes to cast members for the run of the show, and he nearly lost it right there in the studio. "You can't do that," he said. "You have Negroes in the cast. We haven't had a Negro in a fifty-mile radius of this town in a hundred years, and we're damn proud of it! You can place the whites in homes, but you'll never get a person in this town to put anyone black in their home."

I was so shaken by this statement that I went back to my hotel and cried for an hour. I had never encountered this type of prejudice before. I had been raised in a lily-white town and knew about the trouble between blacks and whites, but I didn't really understand the depth of the division and unrest. There was a bridge between my hometown and the city of Akron, and the valley underneath it was considered "the ghetto." Most of the black people in the area lived there, and it was not a place we visited. But it was what it was, and I had accepted it.

It wasn't until I joined Up with People that I had lost sight of color. I believed we were all the same. Clearly, especially in the South, it was not true. What was I going to do? I had to place the cast members in homes. I called the director, and he said, "It's not the first time this has happened. Just place them in a hotel."

One of the most meaningful songs in our show was "What Color Is God's Skin?": "It is black, brown, yellow / It is red / It is white / Everyone's the same in the good Lord's sight." I believed every word.

What was I going to tell our black cast members? These people were my friends! What would happen when the buses pulled in, and everyone got off, and the hosts were standing there with their cards raised with cast members' names on them? After a while, all the white people would leave, and all the black people would be left standing by the buses. Surely, they'd look around at each other and figure it out. Some of them might have experienced it before, but it was a real awakening for me, and I got angry.

This was what they lived with all their lives. This battle had been happening for hundreds of years. I had been so protected in my youth that it wasn't until the miniseries *Roots* that I began to understand. That miniseries affected me deeply, but here I was with this horrific prejudice sitting in front of me. Besides, what qualified as black? Just the American blacks? We had Africans and Panamanians, Puerto Ricans and Mexicans, Jamaicans and Dominicans. How dark could someone be and still be "acceptable" to people in towns like this?

I didn't sleep all night. Finally, morning came, and I went on the radio show. "We have cast members from all over the world," I said, "and this is your chance to meet people from somewhere else—from another place, from another country, from another background. Take this chance to learn and grow and do something great with your life and your kid's life. It will be the opportunity of a lifetime. You choose. We have people from Panama, Belgium, Africa, Switzerland, Jamaica, France, Puerto Rico, Mexico, Italy, Germany, the Dominican Republic, Spain, and across the USA. We have American Indians, black Americans, Irish Americans, and Italian Americans, tall, short, fat, and thin Americans. Grow. Learn. Live. Change your life. It will be fun, educational, and exciting."

We placed every single member of the cast and crew. I never told the unsuspecting members of the cast what had happened. The rest of the group arrived in town, I joined the show, and we gave our usual performance. I doubt we changed the town forever. I'm sure no miracles occurred. But I'd like to think we affected the people there for a while, and maybe some of them for a little longer.

# Fifteen

*I want to spend some time discussing Moral ReArmament and Up with People as a cult and how it affected me.* During this experience, I was subject to emotional highs and lows. Being indoctrinated into a way of life with moral undertones overcrowded my already teeming head. I saw the world, but at what price? The excitement of traveling, the crazy odds of being accosted in a cathedral, and the in-your-face racism that I had never experienced before were all intertwined with this altruistic message based on a religious sect formed long before I stepped onto that bus.

It was in 1938 that, under the spiritual leadership of American minister Frank Buchman and his Oxford Group, the religious sect Moral ReArmament was formed. They believed that God would rule the world through direct communication with humankind. They lived by the high standards of "absolute purity, absolute honesty, absolute unselfishness, and absolute love." Since Up with People was, in its formative years, a faction of MRA, we shared those same absolute standards on the road. There was no dating, or you'd be sent home, no drugs, or you'd be sent home, and homosexuality was forbidden and was a surefire way to be put on a plane.

There are many well-known people who came out of the Up with People/Moral ReArmament experience, including entertainers, directors, musicians, and industry leaders. One of my castmates, award-winning actress Glenn Close, has called it a cult. In an interview with *The Hollywood Reporter*, she revealed that her father, a doctor who had spent years in the Congo battling Ebola, decided to join a "religious cult, Moral ReArmament. What began as an anti-war movement gradually turned into a possessive, all-consuming and exclusionary force." When Glenn's family became involved with the movement, she was removed from her beautiful Connecticut home, and she, her brother, and her sisters were sent to live at the group's headquarters in Switzerland, where she was immersed in the tenets of this cult. She states, "I didn't see my father for a year." Later, she was sent to a boarding school, but that didn't keep her from being drawn into her family's complete obsession with the group and its absolute moral standards. She states, "If you talk to anybody who was in a group that basically dictates how you're supposed to live and what you are supposed to say and how you are supposed to feel, from the time you're seven until the time you're twenty-two, it has a profound impact on you." Her father chose to immerse her family in a religious sect whose teachings would affect her for years. She, too, was an unsuspecting child.

Another alum, award-winning director John Gonzales, says, "It's important to remember that in 1968 we disassociated ourselves from MRA and became Up with People Incorporated, a separate entity, removing ourselves from the baggage of MRA. I feel it was indeed a cult during its first decades. My feeling is that anyone who suffered family dysfunction or were disillusioned by the evolution that marked that MRA era can have sincere convictions of having been brainwashed or captured by a cult. Those of us, from 1968 on, were part of a movement, a dream, and an adventure … but certainly not a cult."

I didn't *feel* like I was part of a cult. We didn't encourage marriage to children, torture, beatings, or shunning. Yet I must admit, I left feeling brainwashed.

I'd spent most of my growing-up years very confused. Sexually, I knew way more than the ordinary kid because of my discussions with my dad. On the other hand, I had the Catholic Church and my mother breathing down my neck with their view that sex was only for procreation, and now Moral ReArmament was preaching its own intense, restrictive standards. Yet Moral ReArmament and Up with People made me feel at peace. I was doing something important. I never wanted to be anywhere else. I was living the life I was meant to live. I was singing and dancing, out there doing my solos in front of a crowd, sending my songs out to touch people's hearts and lives, and feeling the applause coming right back to me. I was happy—until I left. Then the moral code we lived by in Up with People and the beliefs we held blurred with the real world outside of that bubble.

The passion to change the lives of our generation and to be a better person stayed with me for a long time and affected me both positively and negatively in the years to come. I felt immense gratitude for having been able to travel and learn much about our world mixed with a great amount of anger over the cultish influence. One thing that I never stopped feeling was love for the cast and crew with whom I spent four years. We were a family. We had grown up together. We had shared a common youth, and no matter who we were, whom we turned into, whether we became someone special or were just one of the crowd, it didn't matter. We all had a story in common, and that story had bound us together for life.

We had been drawn into this group together in the hope of changing the world, but more than anything, *it changed us.*

# $\mathcal{S}$ixteen

*In the glorious haze of Up with People and the great life we were living,* I became more susceptible to the group's message on dating and marriage. There was no dating, but almost magically, there were engagements. A male member of the cast, usually one of the higher-ups in the Moral ReArmament leadership, would receive guidance that he was to marry someone else within the group. (I'm not sure if that was true or if management just wanted us to think that if we hadn't received guidance about something, it was a no-go.) The person would then seek the blessing of the executive director before making the proposal.

It seemed like destiny for them to have this revelation and blessing in choosing their partner. As an impressionable young girl with a predilection for fantasy, I hoped that one day this would happen to me. It was thrilling when a couple would announce their engagement onstage during a rehearsal to whooping and celebrating from the cast. What I didn't know was that there was an ulterior motive in these matches. If it was good for the company, then it was good for the show and, consequently, good for you.

I did fall in love with a member of the cast during this time and, without a single date, married him. He has not given me his permission to discuss our life together, so I will respect that and tell you about things that happened from my perspective only.

I was so happy and head over heels in love. Unfortunately, the powers that be in UWP were not pleased. Despite all their talk about equality between people and love of people, whoever they were, this match tested their true belief system. After this union, there was no coming back into the fold. There would be no returning to the life I had loved for so many years.

Beginning a new life outside the UWP bubble was an awakening. I was living in a new home as a young wife in beautiful Santa Fe, New Mexico, so far across the country from my family and friends. I was happy yet confused. This was not what I had planned. I had wanted to be a "lifer." I had wanted to stay with UWP, to remain committed to the cause for life. I had to try to figure out who I was. I was a mixed-up mess, a kid who knew nothing about the real world—not a formula for a successful marriage. Not only that, but many of the rules I had lived by in UWP did not work in the outside world. One of those, absolute honesty, was never going to work in the broad public spectrum. Back when I was traveling, some of the girls had come up to me and said they needed to "get honest" with me. This meant they were going to tell me how they thought I was behaving badly. In these scenarios, you were supposed to listen to what someone said and make changes to your life. The girls said that I used to sit with them and have lunch with them, but since I had become "a big star" with the show, I no longer paid them any attention. They were right, and I made a point to spend more time with these dear girls.

In the real world, you cannot go up to someone and tell them what they are doing wrong in their life and expect them to change. You'll get a strong "Eff off!" The outside world has not been programmed to respond kindly to that kind of confrontation.

I had no specific goals. I had no passion to "become" anything. It had all been taken away. Now I had to concentrate on being an adult, get a job, and go back to school part-time. I took general courses because I had no idea what I wanted to do. I just felt that I needed an education to do anything. I figured I would figure it out as I went along. I also knew how my father expected me to act as a married woman, but again, finding reality in his words of wisdom was hard to achieve.

I was a certified school bus driver for a while. Don't laugh! It's true. Learning to maneuver that vehicle was a challenge I couldn't resist. I loved my young schoolchildren and took the responsibility seriously.

Then I got a job in the evenings working for National Car Rental at the airport. It was fun meeting so many different people, and though the work itself was not very interesting, I was bringing home a paycheck. I didn't have a lot of friends in my new surroundings, so when my boss asked a few of us to his house for dinner, I was excited to go. It would be great to meet some coworkers and create new friendships. I was stunned to arrive and find out that it was an Amway meeting! Amway (short for American Way) was a business that sold health and beauty products. It was a pyramid scheme, but not an illegal one. It came close, but in 1979 the Federal Trade Commission found that it passed muster because it did sell physical products and pay for recruitment. As an Amway representative, you sold products, and someone above you received part of your commission. You then recruited new people who also sold products, and you got some of their commission. Not only was I not interested in becoming involved with this company, I also was angry that I had been misled into thinking that I was going to a social dinner. I quit the job.

Like a miracle, the heavens parted, and a few of us who had been deemed outcasts were invited to return to Up with People. This time, I would be a codirector of a cast that would take a group on a tour of the Southwest and Mexico. I knew that was where I was meant to be, doing what I was meant to do. I was happy and safe again. Getting back on the road was healing and exhilarating.

I have forgotten many of the specifics of that tour, but I remember performing in Acapulco. It was a beach town with spectacular hotels surrounded by abject poverty. I have seen this all over the world. The owners made a fortune while the staff scraped by.

After that tour, a smaller group of thirty-five from the cast was invited to Japan, sponsored by Pepsi. I had long wanted to go to this beautiful country and was thrilled to have the opportunity to perform there. Starting in April 1971, we spent six weeks performing in Sapporo, Sendal, Maebashi, Nagano, Kanazawa, Kyoto, Hiroshima, Kumamoto, Fukuoka, Takamatsu, Osaka, Tokyo, and Nagoya. We even recorded a record! Japan was full of culture, precious children, polite people, and tradition. As often as possible, we were assigned to the home of a Japanese family. There I discovered so much about Japanese people's way of life, their customs, and their generosity. I remember being invited to take a bath in my host family's home one evening. I walked into a large room covered in tile. I sat on a stool and washed down before entering the communal tub. You had to be perfectly clean before getting in. It was an honor to be the first one to bathe, and I stepped into a tub of steaming-hot water. It was so incredibly hot that after soaking for only a few minutes, I got out, and my skin was a vibrant red! Then I went off to my room, where I slept on a rice pillow, covered with a soft down comforter, and had the best sleep of my life. One thing I learned was not to admire anything specific in a family's home. You had to be careful not to say you loved something in particular, or they would give it to you! This happened to me when I admired a Japanese doll the family had on a shelf. The mother of the family immediately handed it to me. "For you to remember us," she said. This touched me so much that I took off the fringe suede vest I was wearing, which was very popular at that time, during the hippie phase of our generation, and gave it to them. "For you to remember me," I said.

This was one of my favorite trips, and Japan would remain one of my favorite countries. Being the codirector of a group was a huge responsibility. I did my best to make the cast feel like normal young people and not over-indoctrinated.

While in Hiroshima, the cast went to the Memorial Peace Museum, dedicated to documenting the atomic bombing of the city by our country during World War II. It was horrifying. There was a large table with a ball hanging down over a mock-up of the city. Long, thin sticks protruded from the ball to show the distance the explosion had covered. I saw melted spoons and bicycles, tattered and burned clothing, and photos that will never leave my mind. I wanted to pull my hat down over my eyes. My heart hurt for them.

Later, on our way home, we stopped in Hawaii and visited the USS *Arizona* Memorial. I remember feeling the same shock and hurt I had felt in Hiroshima, only this time it was for the American soldiers who had lost their lives. Perhaps my prior experience with Up with People was too vivid in my mind, because I was laid-back as a director. In this small group, kids were permitted to form relationships and even smoke (can you imagine my gall?). Word got back to the company, and I was asked to leave the show again. Boom, I was out. No need for a rebellious director who just wanted kids to lead a normal life.

So I moved back to my home state of Ohio and settled into an apartment on Independence Avenue, not chosen for its name but appropriate. Talk about culture shock! It was the beginning of the end of my marriage and an ache that would last forever.

My parents' marriage had been difficult in so many ways. They had stayed together because their church demanded it. I had grown up with that unfortunate example and swore that it would never happen to me. No one had any way of knowing that I had come into this marriage with a mindset that if things got bad, or if we weren't happy, I would leave. I only knew that I wasn't going to stay married if I was miserable. It wasn't something I could say out loud, but I felt it in my heart. I take responsibility for that. It was my decision based on a past that was full of confusion.

I take the blame for the mess that I made of this relationship. There were so many things I didn't understand about my childhood. Had I known, it might have changed so many things about my future.

We were married at nineteen and a half and divorced by twenty-one. I stayed in Ohio, settling back into my black-and-white life. I never wanted to see or hear about the show again after that.

# $\mathscr{S}$eventeen

*After my divorce, I moved back in with my mom and dad. It was like* stepping back in time. I had been all around the world and now found myself back at home once again, with two deeply religious, conservative Catholics. I was sent to meet with the monsignor, who informed me that in the eyes of the church, I was still married. I was not to date or be seen with a man in any compromising situation. I could, however, get an annulment, and then all would be right with God and the church. An annulment would make it as though the marriage had never occurred. It was ridiculous, but my parents insisted. So with $500 in hand, I went before a tribunal that wanted to know every detail of my marriage so that they would feel better about a decision that I already had gone through agony to make. Annulment received.

I felt a sense of loss and helplessness as to what I was supposed to do with the emotions and memories that I wasn't allowed to talk about but that were very much a part of my life. I had to pretend that the marriage had never happened. We all just went on. In keeping with family tradition, we never spoke about that blip in my life again.

I was a twenty-one-year-old divorcée. I was certain I was to blame for the inadequacies that had turned my marriage from dream to devastation in record time. I think my family thought so too. Living at home, I was dealing with my own loss and the suffering of my family. Their hurt over my divorce seemed almost as great as mine, and they were struggling with what to do with this daughter who had let them down. My parents' own marriage had endured a great deal. They must have wondered how their daughter could have given up so easily. We never discussed the details. I simply told them I was coming back, and they took me in.

My family told me not to date, even after the annulment. They weren't ready. I was twenty-one, and I was done for. But I didn't want to go out anyway. I just wanted to stay home and lick my wounds. Besides, my father had already warned me, "Men will expect that you'll be looking for sex, now that you are divorced."

"Why is that, Dad?" I asked.

"Because they'll figure that you've been having sex on a regular basis and you'll want it again," he told me.

"Ah, OK," I answered. Good to know. It was a strange message, coming from Dad. I didn't quite grasp what he was really saying, but there was so much more to what he was telling me than what I heard. At any rate, I let it slide. The last thing I planned to do was go out on the prowl and find a guy. I figured sex wasn't my strong suit, or I'd still be married.

I had to get a job, any job—just something to get me out

of the house. I had no education except a semester of college and nothing to use as a reference. Singing and dancing didn't qualify me for much. I needed a purpose. *Get up, get out of bed, keep breathing, don't feel sorry for yourself, and go to work*, I told myself. Going to college to study theater was out.

My father soon realized the folly of my living at home, so he purchased a duplex a few blocks away. Mom was great with money. After growing up without any, she had saved and saved as an adult. Dad had become a manager, had added the sale of Maseratis at the dealership, and now had older customers bringing their children to him for cars. As his income had risen, Mom had taken the increase and saved it. I never thought about their using their savings for me. In my mind, it was just one more thing that my dad did to make me happy. I doubt I even said thank you to Mom, but I sure hope I did. I moved into the first floor of the duplex, and eventually a woman named Cam moved in upstairs. She was a single mom with a six-year-old, towheaded, blue-eyed boy with whom I fell in love immediately. Cam and I formed a friendship that began with our sharing our upstairs-downstairs lives and her beautiful son, and our friendship lasts to this day.

I finally got a secretarial job. It was boring, but it was work, which was what I needed.

Months later, I realized that being who I was, there was no way I was going to listen to any advice about not dating. I thought I'd dip my toe back into the pool, but I was unprepared for the huge splash it would make. Though I had dated in high school, that had been Catholic dating. Not much happened sexually other than heavy kissing. I knew the way to a man's heart was through sex, but I knew I was not supposed to actually have sex without the approval of my religion, my father, and God. I was trying to be part of my generation where, as the song said, "making love was just for fun," while remaining a good girl.

During the Vietnam War, many of us wore prisoner of war bracelets. I ran into someone who actually knew my former POW. I made arrangements to meet him in a town not too far away. I wanted him to know how we had all thought of him every day, how courageous he was, and how proud of him we all were. We spent a day and a night together. We talked and talked and talked. Clearly, he had been through so much. We made gentle love and held each other as we slept. The next day, he started talking about marriage and family. He was ready to get going on the life he had missed. Though I liked him a lot, I was not ready to accept his offer to move down to his place so we could begin a relationship. I softly let him know that I wasn't ready. Perhaps I had unintentionally misled him by coming to see him. I felt terrible as I left, wishing him all the happiness in the world.

A few months later, some friends wanted to go out to a "hippie farm" for some fun. All sorts of colorful people were having a cookout, and we started talking with them. As we sat there, one of them handed me a bong. "Hash," he said. I'd never tried drugs before. It was the early seventies, and everyone in my generation was dabbling in drugs.

"Uh, thanks," I said. Why not? I was getting an education in things I had previously known nothing about. I inhaled the magic, and my lips felt numb. However, I did feel remarkably happy. I walked over to the barn and climbed up to the hayloft, where there was an open door. I sat with my legs hanging over the edge and took in the panoramic view. I felt so light as I sat there dangling my legs that I thought, *I wonder how it would feel to just scoot off of the edge and float down to the ground.* Thankfully, I didn't do that, but I did make the decision later that evening that perhaps I should stay away from drugs. I was far too susceptible to that type of euphoria.

I went out with two different guys (not at the same time) who were so appealing to look at. In both cases, we had been dating for a month or so when the guy said, "Oh, by the way, I've had a long-term relationship for years. I've been trying to decide if I should marry this person, but I met you and wanted to see if this was a possibility." I kid you not. I was some sort of litmus test to see if they were really committed to their relationships or not. Apparently, I didn't measure up. One even said, "Being with you is like slipping on a comfortable pair of slippers." What? Did that mean the other girls were Jimmy Choos? Was I not pretty or glamourous enough? Were they better at sex? Was I just some attractive hausfrau? Why did I keep walking into these same relationships? No, it was more than that. I'd jump right in with an open heart, never thinking to keep a distance or ask more questions, expecting too much from too little a source. What was wrong with me?

I decided to try the "slow-down" method of dating—take it easy, don't rush in so fast.

I met a very nice guy, just a good person, and we went out on three dates. It was nothing intimate—dinners, talking, getting to know each other. On the third date, he took me to a beautiful home he was building and asked me to marry him. "All this can be yours. You can pick out all the finishes." Apparently, the slow-down method didn't work even without sex. I graciously thanked him and said I wasn't ready.

# Eighteen

*There was a big brokerage firm across the hall from my office, and every* day through the glass doors, I would watch the men in their smart-looking suits, shined shoes, and very businesslike briefcases as they came and went through the glass doors that led to the mysterious world of stocks and bonds. It seemed so glamorous and exciting from the vantage point of the desk where I worked. *They* were doing something important, something that took brains and skill. They were dealing with the economy and wealth; I was struggling with carbon paper and rough-edged erasers.

One day, a pleasant-looking man from across the hall came into my dreary little world and spoke to me. His bright eyes and smiling face were a relief. We struck up a friendship, and I looked forward to his stopping in to say hello and chat for a while when he had a moment. He treated me as though I was an actual person, rather than a placeholder behind a typewriter. By the time he asked me to lunch a month or so later, we were old pals, and we laughed and talked easily. He was older than I had first thought. He was thirty-two, and he was married with two kids. He could be like an older brother, I thought. We had lunch often, and I appreciated his friendship.

Over lunch, I began to confide in him the things I had not been able to share with my parents and friends. I told him about my marriage and about my belief that I must have failed my husband in some way. I told him about being "comfortable slippers" and that I wanted to be Jimmy Choos. He was kind and understanding. He listened without recrimination. He offered encouragement and support and was confident that my future held great things. He also offered to become my "teacher."

In my shattered state, all semblance of sanity left me in the hopes of becoming worthy of being loved. And so my lessons began. We gave up our lunches and drove to his home each day. While his wife worked, we spent our time in their bed, where I learned everything from the gentle, slow intricacy of foreplay to the spice of finding ways and places to have sex.

My lessons lasted for a few months. I think the curiosity, drama, mystery, and intrigue pretty much played themselves out. I had learned all I wanted to, and it was starting to feel creepy. I began to wonder if he really was this caring person who wanted to help me or if he was using me. Extricating myself from that situation was tricky, but I managed. I even remember thanking him. Never let it be said that I hadn't been taught my manners.

I did learn some things, funny as that sounds, but all of them were technical. It was like going to school to learn about plumbing. There was something missing in what I was trying to do. I just didn't know what it was.

I knew that I had to stop acting crazy and simply take my time. I needed to slow the heck down and stop obsessing over something I couldn't control. Just take one day at a time, I told myself.

I was invited to an upscale social event through some friends and was looking forward to nothing more than a nice, enjoyable evening of dinner and meeting new people. During that event, a couple that I knew came over and introduced me to a very successful friend of theirs. The man was tall, nice-looking, and magnetic. He ended up sitting at my table, and we connected immediately. I was just enjoying the evening. Then, at the end of the night, he asked if he could take me to dinner. He was older than I was, but that didn't faze me. I thought he was great.

We made plans to go out that Saturday, so of course I bought a new dress. It was a simple sleeveless black dress, and I wore white pearls for an accent. I picked out a nice pair of black heels. I couldn't afford Jimmy Choo heels, but these were an attempt to look more sophisticated, more grown-up, more stylish. My hair was no problem. It was long and had a natural wave. I was ready ahead of time and tried to stay cool while I waited for him to arrive.

Cam kept running down to check on my progress. We laughed and smoked cigarettes and kept peeking out the window until my date finally pulled into the driveway and stepped out of his flashy sports car. Cam was knocked out by the whole package, him and the car.

I opened our communal front door, and there he was, smiling his beautiful smile.

"Ready?" he asked.

"You bet," I answered. And off we went.

The restaurant was elegant and expensive. He held out

my chair as I sat and treated me like a fine piece of china that might break if he weren't gentle with me. *This is nice*, I thought. *Just take your time.* We began getting to know each other. He seemed so much more mature than most of the guys I knew, and he was easy to talk to and laugh with. He was such a real man! He was also full of compliments about how nice I looked and how glad he was to be with me. He liked boating, and so did I. There has always been something about the water that calms my mind. My family had a boat for a while when I was a kid, but Mom hated it. She didn't like the way it bounced around on the water or the way it messed up her hair, so Dad eventually got rid of it.

We talked about his job and my job. I was a complete novice in the business world in comparison to this go-getter. I didn't mention my past. No one would understand UWP unless they were in it, and it meant nothing now anyway.

I told him that I had started attending night school. I was going places too, in a blind sort of way. I couldn't afford to pay for college. If there were student loans back then, I didn't know about them. I wasn't smart enough for a scholarship, and my family certainly couldn't afford to pay for my education. The company would pay for school if I studied business, so I had given up my theater dreams and was taking some business courses. I got As in accounting and liked the order that went with it.

My date drank whiskey throughout dinner, and I drank iced tea. I wasn't much of a drinker. We talked about politics, and I heard more about his life. I liked him. He was different.

There were stars in my eyes that night, and I didn't really pay attention as he drank one Jack Daniels after another. After dinner, he asked if I'd like coffee. Unsure if he wanted to get going, I asked what he'd prefer. He said he was having another

Jack, so I had coffee, and we laughed and talked some more. What a great time we were having!

"I like you," he said.

"I like you too," I answered back, sure I was on the road to happiness.

I understood social drinking. Every day of his adult life, my father drank one Seven and Seven (Seagram's Seven and 7 Up) and ate one square of Hershey's chocolate, not at the same time. (He lived into his nineties, so I'm pretty sure he discovered the secret of youth.) Mom rarely drank. She liked both amaretto and white zinfandel, but she didn't handle either well. Whenever we could, my sister and I would slip her an extra glass just to watch her get the giggles. What I didn't understand was the changes alcohol could bring to the personality of a person.

As my date was driving me home, he said he needed to stop by his house to pick up something. We pulled up in front of a fabulous home and went inside.

He put on some music and went to pour another Jack for himself and a glass of wine for me. We talked while I looked around. It was a beautiful place. He was clearly good at what he did.

He returned with our drinks, and we talked for a while more. Then he came over and kissed me. *Hmm, good kisser,* I thought. *A very good kisser.* Then he started getting playful, and I laughed self-consciously. I wanted him to like me. I liked his kisses. Clearly, I liked him a lot. But I wasn't sure if I wanted more on this first date. I was on the slow-down plan. I figured if I just explained, he'd understand.

"Wait, maybe we should—" I began, but he was getting into it. How could I get out of this gracefully?

What? What was he saying? He really, really liked me.

"I like you too, but we need to take this a little slower," I said. I didn't want to get into my past relationship issues. That would seem childish. Besides, he'd been drinking, and he didn't seem too levelheaded now. This wasn't the time for a long, heartfelt talk. "We have plenty of time to get to know each other," I said. "Let's go on a few more dates to see if this is where we want this to go."

"We need to see if we're sexually compatible," he said through his kisses. "Otherwise, what's the point?"

I hadn't heard that one before. I found him immensely physically appealing, and I didn't want to come off like some child. I was in a miserable situation, and I didn't know how to handle it. This was the coolest guy in the world. I was just some inexperienced kid. I had to get control—quick!

His kisses reeked of alcohol. I hated the smell of him. It was time to go. "I think you should take me home," I said with as much firmness as I could muster.

"No, not yet," he pleaded. "Come on, baby."

"Really," I said, "I think it's time. I'm not ready for this."

"I care about you, more than you know. I want you so much. I need you. I need you to stay," he said.

He unzipped my dress and unhooked my bra at almost the same time. I could hardly believe it. How did guys do that?

"Please, not tonight," I said, trying to get myself back together.

"Baby, you are the one for me. I need you so much." He was kissing me and taking off his shirt and getting kind of rough. I struggled and tried to push him away, trying to use my logic while my mind was going double-time.

Then he picked me up, all 108 pounds of me, carried me into his bedroom, and plopped me on his bed. In a second, he was on top of me.

"Please, don't do this," I begged.

"You know you want to," he answered. It's amazing how a man can get his pants and your underwear off while completely inebriated and still hold you down without missing a beat.

It was pointless to struggle. I thought it would be better just to get through it. My mind started wandering. I had been hoping for romance. This wasn't romance. Maybe it was my own fault. I had wanted him, and here I was. Why wasn't I just jumping in and enjoying every moment?

This wasn't the way I had wanted it to be, that's why. Because it wasn't my idea. It could be worse. This wasn't some rapist in a dark alley. He didn't have a knife. He wasn't about to kill me. People had lived through much worse situations. Who was I? No one. Just some stupid girl. This was my own fault. Dumb, dumb, dumb girl.

Anyway, I couldn't fight him. It seemed best to just relax— if only I could relax. I told myself to just endure it until it was over. My God, was there no end? Maybe it was the alcohol. Maybe that's what was making it take so long. I lay there naked on his bed while he sweated and breathed his Jack-thick breath all over me. I waited and looked at his popcorn ceiling. I hate popcorn ceilings. They're so hard to paint.

Finally, he fell exhausted at my side, his arm draped over me. I dared not wake him.

In the movie *Coyote Ugly*, Maria Bello's character, Lil, is asked why she named her restaurant "Coyote Ugly." She answers: "Did you ever wake up sober after a one-night stand, and the person you're next to is lying on your arm, and they're so ugly you'd rather chew off your arm than risk waking 'em? That's coyote ugly."

I sort of felt that way, only the man next to me wasn't ugly. He was still incredibly handsome. When I woke up there the next morning, he said, "Good morning, beautiful," as though nothing unusual had happened.

When he took me home, I told him that I didn't think the relationship would work. "I'm more of a 'comfortable pair of slippers' kind of girl," I said. He looked at me like I had two heads. And that was that. I stopped dating for a while and decided to concentrate on my job.

# Nineteen

*Predators are out there, everywhere, hiding in the most upright, upscale,* suit-and-tie jobs. You can't tell who they are by the way they look or how they dress, whom they're married to, or whom they know. You can't pick them out of a crowd, and nothing prepares you for them. But predators are predators are predators. It's a good word. It has that cloak-and-dagger feel to it, and that's how they act: lurking in the shadows, waiting to jump out on unsuspecting girls (or boys) and women (or men) so they can abuse without being caught. Then they jump back into society, where they're seen as respectable, keeping their dark, dirty little secrets for themselves.

Professionals, especially, seem to hide behind the respectability mask. I had two doctors who couldn't seem to examine me without pushing their hard-ons into my side. I kept changing doctors in the hope of finding a decent medical professional who wasn't looking for a kick. I found one in the form of a young, handsome, married guy with two little children. I loved going to him. His energy and manner were refreshing. One day, I went to book an appointment with him, and the nurse said he wasn't practicing at their facility anymore. I liked him and wanted to keep going to him. I decided to Google him to find out where he was. He had been arrested. He had been part of a large child pornography ring. He wouldn't be practicing anywhere. I was crushed. Here was a talented man who had given up years of schooling, a wife, and a family. He had let them down. He had let himself down. He had let all of us down.

I was doing well at the place where I worked, and I asked for more and more responsibilities. They decided to send me to a branch office to receive management training. My new boss was a classy guy with a sophisticated, well-regarded wife. They were prominent socially, and I was a little in awe of them. My job kept me busy learning something new each day. I was working with a lot of men and wanted to prove my worth to them. I was smart enough to learn the ropes of the job and knew that I could succeed as well as any of the guys on the team if I kept my wits about me and worked with all my energy. I'd been there for about six months when my boss said he'd like to take me to lunch to discuss the "amazing" work I'd been doing. Heck, he took everyone to lunch, but I was still thrilled. He was "impressed," he said.

"You have a real way with people. You're smart, and I think you can go places. Let's talk about it over lunch."

Wow. That was music to my ears. These lunches were how it worked in business. Guys got together and discussed business. Bosses found young protégés and, over business lunches, discussed their future. This was going to be great!

"I'd love to," I said.

We left at noon and got into his Cadillac. Cadillacs were huge back then, like boats. This was fun, and I wanted to own one of my own someday. We drove to the next town and pulled into an A&W Root Beer stand. It was not exactly the place I had been expecting for a business meeting from this classy guy with this classy car, but hey, business meetings could happen anywhere, right? I wondered if this was where he took the guys too. Anyway, I figured we could talk in the car over hamburgers and root beer floats as easily as we could over a table with chairs.

He pulled the car way into the back of the lot, near some trees. That seemed a little strange, but I didn't say anything. The carhop came over and took our order. We talked for a while about how I liked my job, and I think I was in the middle of a sentence when he unzipped his pants and pulled out the biggest, most erect penis that had ever been gifted to man.

"Impressive, isn't it?" he asked.

I was speechless. This was my boss! This was an important guy! This was ... his poor wife!

"Do you want to touch it?" he invited.

Oh my God. "No!" I exclaimed.

"Go ahead," he said. "It's OK. I won't tell anyone."

Was he kidding? "I don't want to touch it. Put it away!"

"Are you sure?" he asked, still sitting there with his penis hanging out like a flag in the wind. "You're making a mistake."

Where was the carhop? You can never get a root beer float when you really need one! I just sat there, looking out my window like a mute dolt while he somehow forced that thing back into his pants.

We sat in silence, and he smoked a cigarette until our order came. He tried to make small talk while he ate, and I tried to eat and talk as well.

When we got back to the office, he cautioned me, "I wouldn't mention this to anyone."

No mention of my evaluation. No mention of his penis. I did, however, get a nice raise. (No pun intended.)

*

# Twenty

*This was a time when victims of predators stayed silent, fearful of re-*percussions. It was 1972, and the Clarence Thomas and Anita Hill hearings hadn't yet put sexual harassment on the map. What we learned from Anita Hill was that she took too long to speak out. She wasn't believed. This was long before the #MeToo movement helped all of us who were victims learn to speak up.

I was among the sexually scarred who stayed silent, who stored our abuse in the subconscious recesses of our brains. Then one day, we close our eyes, and the beast of the past jumps out. I say, kill the beast.

There are other stories, ridiculous relationships, and encounters that, if I were to repeat them, would simply become redundant. Once you have faced abuse as many times as I have in my life, you are simply no longer able to recognize it.

I hit the papers looking for work. I finally took a job as a full-charge bookkeeper for two decent, married, kind men who owned their own business. I was doing work that appealed to the analytical side of my brain, and I got to use the years of accounting courses I had completed.

However, bookkeeping is dry. There's no soul. It wasn't the breath of air I sorely needed. So I did the only thing I could do: I went back to performing in the theater at night.

# Twenty-one

*One of the great things about being in the theater is that it doesn't* matter who you are or where you've been or what your private life is like. What's important is who you are onstage and what you give while you're there. Show up on time, know your lines, and give a hundred percent of yourself to your character and to the other performers, and that's all that matters. That always appealed to me. Trying to explain anything about my life, especially my time on the road, was too hard. Though it had been fun and exciting, no one really understood it. You had to be there. No one really cared. It didn't mean anything to anyone back home, and I had gone back to being no one again. I worked a black-and-white job and led a black-and-white life. It was more fun being someone else onstage and forgetting about real life for a while. I liked living someone else's drama or doing a comedy and hearing the audience laughing and getting those good endorphins going. Make the audience feel better, and you'll feel better. Play the play, and we'll all go for a ride for an evening.

If you're a female lead, you get to do a lot of romantic parts, and there is always a handsome young man who has been cast opposite you that you get to kiss. (Most of the time, he's handsome—depends on who's available from the casting call.) This can sometimes be a bonus. In our town and the cities nearby, most of us ended up auditioning for the same shows repeatedly. We got to know each other well, and the same central group of people did most of the shows together. Harold and I did so many plays together that we began to feel like we were related (but not romantically). Not only did we kiss often, but in *Can-Can* I got to slap him too.

A stage slap is all about timing, and the first time I tried it, I was terrified. I'd never slapped anyone, and I couldn't bring myself to do it. I was supposed to slap him as he turned his face at the same time. Though Harold would indeed get a slap, it would not be a hard one, and it needed to work out so that he wouldn't get hurt. It was important to do it right. I was going to be doing this every night. I could smack him in the nose or ear and leave him bloody or unable to hear for a while. Or I could miss him entirely! But first, I had to stop laughing.

My director said, "Go ahead, smack the boy!" But all I could do was laugh! Nerves make me silly.

We finally got it right, and I felt confident that I was a terrific stage slapper. On opening night, when it came time for the slap, Harold forgot to turn his head, and I hauled off and slapped him good. He said it stung like crazy, but it sounded great! We did it right for the rest of the run, but it was never as much fun after that first slap. If only I'd used that slap in real life against other men!

I also got to cry on Harold's shoulder, and occasionally, I'd use him as my dresser. He was tall, so he'd hold up my long, billowy costumes, and I'd slip under them for a quick change. Then he'd lower them, help me in, and zip them up, and off we'd go again.

I remember one night when I had a stuffy nose. We sang our song, which ended with a romantic kiss, and then ran offstage.

Harold said, "Marylee, was that Vicks?"

"What?" I asked.

"As I was kissing you," he said, laughing, "all I could smell was Vicks!"

I'd put some under my nose to keep my sinuses clear so I could sing. The stage kiss is not always romantic.

During *A Little Night Music*, which I performed at the Canton Light Opera, I had a great, showstopping number called "The Miller's Son." Alone together on center stage, another cast member, whom I barely knew, and I were supposed to be having a little picnic. He was to give me a quick kiss and then lie down near me on the blanket as I sang this lilting song. Every night (and I begged him over and over not to do this), he would open his mouth wide and give me the biggest, sloppiest kiss you can imagine. Then he'd lay his head down, and I would have to begin singing with yuck all over my face. All I really wanted to do was take my sleeve and wipe my arm across my mouth, but the show must go on!

Speaking of wet kisses, I always felt sorry for Gary during the run of *Carousel*. Gary played Billy Bigelow, and he was one of the most talented singers and actors with whom I ever shared a stage. I loved to stand offstage while he sang "My Boy Bill" (as did the rest of the cast), totally mesmerized along with the audience. Billy Bigelow, of course, dies during the play. It's a terribly sad scene resulting from a "robbery gone wrong." Julie, the character I played, arrives too late and approaches Billy to say goodbye. I would kneel down next to Gary, overwhelmed by grief, and say, "I love you, Billy. I have always loved you." Tears would roll down my face and fall all over him. Then I'd give him a salty kiss, and he'd have to lie there all wet while Cousin Nettie sang, "You'll Never Walk Alone." Dear, sweet Gary. I'm sorry.

The longest stage kiss I ever had was in *1776*. In the play, Thomas Jefferson is with two of our Founding Fathers, John Adams and Benjamin Franklin, in Philadelphia and has been writing the Declaration of Independence, but Jefferson is distracted and frustrated because he hasn't seen his wife, Martha, in six months. He wants to go home for a visit. John Adams sends for Martha instead, thinking that if Jefferson gets to see Martha, the declaration can be written. When Jefferson does see Martha, he sweeps her into his arms, and they kiss. John Adams and Benjamin Franklin try to talk to them, but Thomas and Martha are lost in their long-awaited kiss. As John tries to speak to them, Thomas turns Martha away. Benjamin Franklin tries to approach them from another side, but they turn in a different direction without interrupting their kiss. As the two men continue to ask questions and try to interrupt, Thomas and Martha turn and turn while kissing and ignore the pesky men. Adams and Franklin eventually give up and leave the stage. It's a wonderful, romantic, and funny scene. And it's technical and awkward! When I was cast in the play, I didn't know the actor playing Thomas Jefferson.

"Hi, I'm Marylee."

"Hi, I'm the guy who's going to kiss you for two minutes while my wife, who plays Abigail, watches from offstage."

OK, geez. No pressure there.

The whole thing had to be blocked (or staged), so we did that first: turn right on this line, turn left on that line, hold, turn right again, turn right again, hold, turn left. Then there would be a turn with a big sweep back for drama. Once we had the blocking down, adding the kiss was next. There's always some laughing when you're doing these things. It's nervous energy and sexual tension all rolled into one.

The director says, "OK, kiss the girl, and let's get that out of the way." Very romantic, don't you think?

We added the kiss to the blocking. Onstage, these moments must look spontaneous, totally unrehearsed, and natural. Everything the actors do has to be done without the audience seeing that we're thinking, or it spoils the fun for them. In this scene Thomas and Martha are in love and have missed each other desperately. They are engaged in a kiss that answers all the longing they have felt while away from each other for months. The laughs belong to John Adams and Benjamin Franklin. What the audience sees are two lovebirds being interrupted by two meddling men. It's the magic of theater.

And if you must know, this actor was a good kisser.

I would by lying if I told you that a stage kiss is always dispassionate and unfeeling. Romance does happen in the theater. It would be impossible for it not to. There are so many reasons that it's the perfect place for chemistry.

First, God-given talent can be enormously appealing. Being onstage with someone who has talent can knock you off your feet. You think that sitting in an audience and seeing someone wildly talented sends chills down your spine? Try standing next to him!

Second, there are the stories themselves. The authors have given us these incredible plays with words that are often poetic. We are allowed the thrill of getting to say these words to each other. The writers have given us situations filled with the most dramatic, heart-wrenching, romantic moments and with dialogue that communicates feelings we, as ordinary people, can only dream of speaking. Their words are full of truths, searing commentary, and the deepest emotions.

Next, an actor gets to become someone else for a few hours. You don't act like someone else; you *are* them. You slip into their skin, and they slip into yours. You are yourself as this other person in their world. You have a past, and they have a past, and you have arrived at their present in your life where their story picks up. Their reality becomes your reality, and it's the truth we all share, audience and cast, for the next few hours. The director has told you what is good and what is awful: "Keep this. Throw that out!" You've rehearsed, you've trusted each other, and you have created a living, breathing group of people who exist as a unit.

Last, there are the costumes and the sets. The designers have created your world for you. You are dressed as a new person, and you step into your new world. You are home.

It's easy, then, if the right person is cast with you, to find that the whole setup is perfect for real romance to happen. How could it not? I once had a director say, "I always cast two people that I can picture in bed together." There you have it. Actors try to keep that line between reality and "stage reality" separate. Most of the time, you have developed such a friendship and camaraderie with each other that you feel as though you're slipping into a warm, comfortable robe when you're with the other person. You are free, then, to fall in love for those hours as those characters in that space in time.

The "kiss," no matter how passionate it looks, is still safe to you, because you know your acting partner is professional in their work and not trying to get you into bed under the guise of a character someone has given them. Sometimes, though, the chemistry is real, and it's impossible to deny. Sometimes, the person touches your heart and soul. You never know, as an audience, when what you are seeing is real or just plain fabulous acting. And we're not telling.

I played leads in *The Male Animal* (Eileen), *Yankee Ingenuity* (Gertrude), *Prisoner of Second Avenue* (Edna), *California Suite* (Diana), and *Talley's Folly* (Sally), for which I won a best actress award at the Weathervane Playhouse in Akron, and many, many other plays. I did local radio commercials and magazine ads and kept working my black-and-white job. A core group of actors, three men and three women, got together and created a musical revue that we called *Broadway, Our Way.* This undeniably talented group of friends and fellow performers did shows all over the city, in malls, in senior citizens' homes, and in a small theater, giving a taste of Broadway to the local area. Theater, in all its forms, helped mend my aching heart.

*My big sister, Kathy and me.*

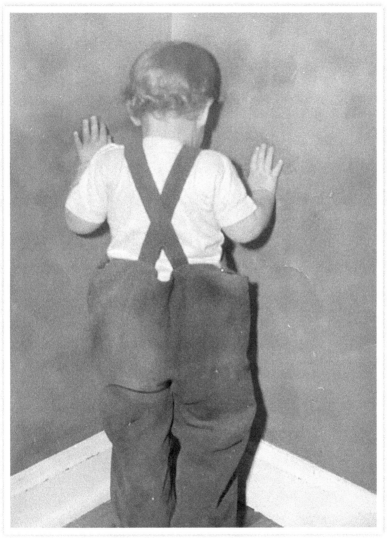

*I don't know what I did, but it must have been really bad!*

*Photos on the wall at Mom and Dad's. Mine is the biggest!!*

*First stage performance. Hooked for life!*

Up with People! *Bob Hope NBC special 1968. I'm in the third row, yellow costume, blonde flipped hair. So much fun.* © Up with People

*Traveling by bus.*

*Solo performance in* UWP.

*Spain! Publicity poster for* Viva La Gente! *That's me in the center with short blonde hair.* © Up with People

*Performing at the Plaza de Toros in Valencia, Spain. Stepping out in front of that crowd to perform my solo was the thrill of a lifetime.* © Up with People

*Meeting with King Baudouin and Queen Fabiola at their Royal Arboretum in Laeken, Belgium. Second Row, second from left.* © Up with People

*Six week tour of Japan sponsored by Pepsi Cola. Small cast toured the country from April -May 1971. I'm the blond in the front, at the center microphone.* © Up with People

The Male Animal *where I played Ellen and got to use my stubborn side.*

*As Connie in* The Big Knife.

*Initial performance of a new musical,* Yankee Ingenuity.
*Loved playing this earnest serving girl.*

*Getting ready backstage for a performance.*

*You can't have more fun than* Can-Can. *I was the sassy, saucy Pistache.*

*One of my favorites, 1776. In this historical and moving musical
I was Martha Jefferson. Here I bantered with John Adams and
Benjamin Franklin singing "He Plays the Violin!"*

*Had a ball with* California Suite *as Diane.*

*Filled a 3,000 seat theater for this production of*
Carousel. *So lucky to play Julie Jordan.*

A Little Night Music *was performed at the Canton Light Opera. I was Petra! Got to knock out the scene stealing song, "The Miller's Son." One of my favorite performances.*

Talley's Folly. *Won a best actress award for portraying Sally in this touching play.*

Summer and Smoke. *It's all about love and loneliness.*
*Tennessee Williams is pure poetry. I was Alma.*

'night, Mother *will always be my favorite play. Jessie was so full of love, hurt, confusion and pain. How could I not identify with her?*

# Twenty-two

*By the time I'd turned twenty-six, my life seemed to have calmed down,* so I went to a party, where I met a quiet, sensitive man. He was tall, blue-eyed, and sandy-haired. We drank and smoked a little weed, and it sure made things funny. We laughed and laughed and talked into the wee hours of the morning. He had a fascinating job as a specialized engineer and traveled a lot. His job was to cover the bow of a ship with a product that would keep barnacles from attaching to it and interfering with the sonar and nuclear devices. He had to go wherever the ship was, and if it was dry-docked, he made the repairs and coated the ship with his company's product. If the ship was in the water, he supervised a team to make underwater repairs. His job was so interesting.

When it was time to leave the party, he said he was going to follow me home to make sure I got there all right. When we arrived, I decided he shouldn't drive any farther. I liked him, and I didn't want to ruin things by sleeping with him, so since Cam wasn't home, I took him upstairs to her apartment and tucked him into her bed.

The next morning, just as I was finishing getting dressed, he came downstairs. While I made us coffee, he joked, "You should have let me sleep with you. I was out the minute I hit the sheets. You would have been as safe as if you were in God's pocket."

He was sweet and soft-spoken, and we talked for several more hours. He was a lot like my dad—smart, kind, handy with tools and woodwork, and a nice, decent person. He had two teenage girls from his first marriage. It felt perfect. I wanted the theater and had almost decided to leave for New York City, but I also wanted to be a mom and a wife.

We dated for a while, and he eventually moved into the duplex with me. I didn't want to make another mistake and decided living together was the answer. Those were the *1776, Pippin, Talley's Folly*, and *Carousel* years. *Carousel* was performed in a 1,500-seat theater, and on opening night there were huge searchlights out front, moving back and forth in the sky. There was a lot of press, and we had many VIP guests. I knew it would be a huge hit. Life was good.

After we had lived together for a while, this dear man asked me to marry him. I loved him, we were happy, and the sex was great. It was all the things I had been promised. Our picture appeared in the society column of our local paper, not because our parents were wealthy, but because I had gained some recognition in the theater, and he was handsome and had a great job.

I knew that marrying him would mean losing any hope of becoming a legitimate actor. I couldn't live in Ohio and audition in New York whenever I wanted. I had responsibilities now. I gave up those dreams (again), and on June 4, 1977, we got married and purchased a beautiful English Tudor home.

His oldest daughter came to live with us. I was thrilled to have a child. She, however, didn't really think that much of me. I was too uppity, too la-di-da, too everything for her. Life got harder. Her dad traveled so much, and that left me, at twenty-seven, in charge of a sixteen-year-old. It was tough for us both, and with my husband away so often, the situation became tense and miserable.

Being a stepparent is tricky. You are not the child's mother, but you are in a position where you need to make the decisions a mother would. We battled, but I loved her. (It took time, but years later, we became so close that I consider her my first daughter.) Her father wasn't much of a heart-to-heart talker. He was a lot like my own dad, come to think of it. To them, it was better just to keep quiet and hope it would all work out.

Then I became the luckiest woman in the world. On January 22, 1980, we had a baby girl whom we named Leigh Anne. She was soft and pink, had tiny dimples, and captured my heart. Her big sister loved being around her and would fly her around in the air just to hear her laugh. She was the center of my happiness, and I loved that I got to be her mommy.

My husband had a biting sense of humor, but I got used to it. I soon discovered, though, that as they say, a lot of truth is said in jest. One day I had just done my hair in a popular curly, frizzy fashion. I asked him if he liked it. "Sure," he said. "Kind of looks like you put your finger in a socket."

Over the next three years, things went sideways. Tensions grew. I was unhappy, and my stepdaughter was unhappy, but Leigh Anne was full of smiles and giggles. My husband was oblivious to what was going on. He was gone so often and didn't really know how to handle the problems at home. I felt like a single parent most of the time. We didn't really know how to communicate, how to talk about our problems, my problems with stepparenting, or anything that needed to be worked on in our marriage.

I was in need of something. Feeling confused about our future, I indulged in the attention I was getting from my friends in the theater. One person in particular had my attention. I spent an afternoon with him, but we both realized it would go nowhere.

My husband was certain I was having an affair. Why else would I be so unhappy? One day, I was on the phone, and it kept clicking and making noise. Every time I used the phone, the same thing would happen. I called the phone company and set up an appointment for someone to come out the next day.

When my husband came home, I told him about the problem and the appointment I had made. He poured a glass of whiskey and went upstairs to take a shower. When he came back down, he said, "You have to call the phone company back. You have to cancel the appointment."

"Why?" I asked.

He replied, "I tapped the phone. That's what's causing the problem."

He took me to the basement to his shop, and sure enough, there was a reel-to-reel recorder set up.

"How long have you been recording my calls?" I asked.

"For a while," he said.

"At least you know I'm not having an affair," I replied as I walked away.

I think I was in shock for a while. My first reaction was to wonder whom I had talked to over the past few weeks. What had I said? What had they said? Family? Friends? I couldn't remember a single thing about any of those calls. But he could.

He knew every word of every call. I felt naked. It would take years for me to understand the complete desperation he must have felt to go to such an extreme.

It felt like the world was closing in on me. With my belief that you shouldn't be married if you weren't happy, I asked for a divorce. I told him I didn't love him anymore and wanted out. He was shocked. He couldn't believe that I wanted to leave.

He told me, "You're taking Leigh Anne." In a million years, I never would have dreamed of leaving her. "You'll be driving some rattletrap car without a dollar to spend," he said, "and you'll come to regret this decision." I did come to regret it later on, as life got harder.

My lawyer advised me to take the house. He said he could get me half of my husband's pension, plus alimony and child support. But I didn't want anything from him. With his first marriage, he had lost the house he had built. I didn't want him to lose everything again. That turned out to be a huge mistake. He gave me child support of $80 a month and a small settlement. Not seeking more had been stupid of me. I had let my emotions get the best of me. My daughter and I were going to be poor, but at least we were free. Leigh Anne was three years old, and I was changing her world.

We moved to a small apartment a few blocks from the house; that way Leigh Anne's father could see her every day if he wanted and take her on weekends when he could.

It was a hard adjustment for my adorable child. She missed her daddy, and it was all my doing. My flirtatious nature, my insecurities, my visions of happily ever after through the eyes of Walt Disney, the influence of my parents' unhappy marriage, and my belief that if things weren't going well, I should leave all had contributed to making this union a mess. I take responsibility for that.

# Twenty-three

*For the next year and a half, I raised my daughter in my black-and-*white world. Stung that I had completely failed at marriage again and hurt that my husband barely spent time with our daughter and that my mom had said no when I asked her to help ("I raised my family—I'm not raising another one"), I packed up everything we owned and headed for the Big Apple. Why not? If her dad wouldn't see her in Ohio, then what difference did it make where we lived? New York was where all my dreams were. I would prove to Leigh Anne that you could pull yourself up by your bootstraps and go after what you wanted in life. I wanted to become an actress. I would show her that a person could accomplish the impossible if they worked hard enough and had enough determination, fire, and passion.

In January 1985, when Leigh Anne was almost five, I began working for a major accounting firm in New York City. I sometimes joked that I did theater only to help pay for my love of accounting (so not true!). The firm was one of the country's "Big Eight." I was happy to have landed a job with such a prestigious firm. Rather than live in the city, however, I set up home in New Jersey, where I felt it was close enough to the city for me to get to work and safe enough to raise my daughter. I had made a decision for her that she had no say in and no control over. The guilt was awful. It was my job to give her a secure home with a mommy and a daddy. I'd contributed to the confusing life of my own little unsuspecting child. I began auditioning on my lunch hour. I was thirty-five years old—too old to start, but never too old to dream.

I loved my job, even if I was doing accounting. I was making pretty good money and had hopes of moving up the ladder. But I would find out that with only an associate's degree, I would be going nowhere.

As for dating, I wasn't beautiful, but I was nice-enough looking. But I had two big drawbacks: I was thirty-five years old, and I had a kid. I was discovering that most men weren't interested in taking on a woman with a child. They wanted to have fun, have great sex, enjoy life, make money, and have no ties. It was a problem. I loved my child and wanted a real home for us, but we managed to have a family of our own together, just the two of us.

We lived in a small apartment in a family-oriented town where they closed down the main street on the Fourth of July for a fair and fireworks. I was leery of raising a child in New York City, so even though commuting from New Jersey was hard and meant longer hours for me, it seemed a better choice to create a more normal existence for my daughter. It meant getting up at five o'clock every morning, making breakfast, getting us dressed and ready by six o'clock, and getting into the car and off to day care by six thirty, followed by a race to the train station. Since I couldn't afford to park in the lot at the station, I'd park several blocks away, grab my briefcase, and literally run to the station to catch the 7:00 a.m. train to New York. The ride took just over half an hour, and then came a dash to the subway, a wait for the number 1 train, the ride uptown, a walk to the office, and a dash to my desk to be seated by eight o'clock to start work.

The job was hectic and demanding, but I liked it. I loved the analytical side of doing taxes and the thought that went into it. I was smart, and I liked thinking through my clients' complex problems. I was learning so much each day, attending seminars and being given increased responsibility. Most of my peers worked until seven at night or later, but I didn't have any choice in that matter. I had to get back home. I had a great boss and had worked out a deal: I'd take work home with me if I could leave at five.

I'd stuff my briefcase with as much work as possible, and while all the guys kept working, I'd head for the door. Off I'd go, down into the subway, awkwardly running in my high heels and suit, with my purse and briefcase swinging. I'd wait for the number 1 train in the stuffy tunnel, hop on the car, and rumble my way to Penn Station. Running again, I'd make my way to the New Jersey Transit section, where I'd catch my breath and the train to my home station. I'd run back to where I'd parked my car several blocks from the station and then drive to the day care center, where my daughter stayed until I got home. Lots of hugs and kisses would ease my guilt over being away, and then we would head home. I'd fix dinner, and we'd play, go outside, go to the park, or color for a while, and then Leigh Anne would have her bath. Finally, it would be her bedtime, and I could start on the work I had carried home from the office.

By eight thirty, I would be all alone. I didn't know a single person in town. Nor did anyone from the city really want to come out to Jersey to spend an evening visiting a mom and her kid. What struck me was how quiet it was after my daughter went to sleep. No one called. No one stopped by. There was total silence. So I worked. I would work until midnight. My boss used to say that I was the only person he knew who would take work home every night and actually do it.

The next day, I'd get up and do it all again, still squeezing in some auditions. I managed to get cast in some commercials (Belmont racetrack, a luxury condo, and some soap work as an extra), and I was lucky to have a boss who let me take the time to do them as long as I got my work done. This went on for years and years and years. It was exhausting. I began to audition less and less. The scenario changed some, of course. My daughter started school, so I had to hire someone to pick her up each day and drive her to a babysitter's house. That took more money from my meager paycheck. After I arrived home, there'd be dance class or gymnastics or softball. Whatever money I could put together went into making her life fun. Bedtime crept to nine, then nine thirty. There were birthday parties and sleepovers, a two-wheel bike to learn to ride, and hair to French-braid or crimp. But still, work would keep me busy until late at night, when I would physically ache with loneliness.

My daughter's world had been upended, and it was my doing. That guilt combined with the financial burden and work responsibilities made my shoulders heavy.

I felt some hope for a while. I met a tall, dark-haired, dark-eyed man, and we began a friendship. He was funny and charming. We started having lunch together, and I liked him a lot. He was divorced as well. He didn't seem intimidated by the fact that I had a daughter, although I was wary of dating yet another person who only wanted a good time. It seemed exhausting. To me, dating meant getting a babysitter for my daughter even though she'd spent all day away from me. I had to really feel that this relationship would be worth the expense and, more importantly, my time away from my child, not to mention her sense of security, just so I could go out for a night. I held off getting involved.

Once my daughter was old enough, during the summer I'd send her back to our hometown in Ohio for a few weeks of summer camp, which she loved. As a child, I had gone to the same camp, and it had been a great experience. There were cabins in the woods, horseback riding, hiking, and greased watermelon contests in the lake where kids tried to grab the melon from each other and carry it back to shore. It's not easy to grab a greased watermelon from someone while someone else is trying to grab it from you. And of course, there were campfires at night where she sang songs while roasting marshmallows on sticks. She even won an award called the Golden Arrow for being the best camper after she took an interest in a special-needs girl. Then she'd go to her grandparents' house for two more weeks, which she loved even more. It gave me a break each year and gave her something to look forward to. It was during that time that I felt free enough to see this truly wonderful man.

Our first date was spectacular. We went to A Dish of Salt, a lovely restaurant in New York City. We enjoyed gourmet cheese, fine food and wine, and an exquisite atmosphere. We laughed and talked and really got to know each other. We spent a lot of time together over the next few weeks, seeing the museums, the theater, and Central Park, savoring life like two single people without a care in the world.

Finally, we had our private time together. How I had missed that! He was warm and passionate, and we were happy. We were more than happy. We were in serious "like." Since we had both been married before, we weren't in a hurry. We were just enjoying being together.

And we were being responsible. At least *I* was being responsible. Men hate condoms. They tend to want women to take care of that sort of thing. We knew all the risks of unprotected sex. We just thought we could outsmart Mother Nature. We were mature and educated. I was using a diaphragm, and I remember saying, as I spread my spermicidal jelly over the rubber device, "You know, you could take responsibility for birth control every now and then."

"You're right," he replied from the other room. But I knew nothing would ever come of it.

I hadn't really been watching for my period. My daughter was back, and I was working. We were on our schedule, and we had a new person in our life who was coming over regularly and including my daughter in our plans. It was perfect.

I remember that I got up from my desk to go to the ladies' room one afternoon, and while I was in there, it struck me that I was late for my period. And then, somehow, I knew instinctively. I could feel it, that slight, distinctive difference in my body. The tiniest of changes that begin within those first few weeks—they were there. I counted backward. Two weeks late. There it was. I returned to my office and sat motionless for a while. I wasn't about to go through this on my own. I called him.

"I need to see you."

We agreed to meet for lunch.

"I may be pregnant," I said.

The color drained from his face. For a moment, he was silent. Then he said, "Are you sure?"

"No," I answered. "But I'm pretty sure."

He visibly struggled with his reply. "What do you want to do?"

"I've just made an appointment with my doctor. I'll let you know," I said.

"OK," he said. "Whatever you decide, I'll stand by you." They were the most welcome words I'd ever heard, but I could see absolute fear in his eyes as he said them.

The doctor was an old-world gentleman, and I expected a long lecture from him after his examination. I already knew what the results were going to be.

"You are pregnant," he said.

"Yes," I answered. I just sat there. "Thank you," I said in a daze.

"You have a small child already, is that not so?" he asked.

"Yes."

"You have a choice not to have this child, you know," he said very gently.

"I'm Catholic," I replied, as if that explained it all.

"Only you can decide what is right for your life," he told me. "I'm not encouraging you to do anything one way or the other. I just want you to know that you have a choice."

I vividly remember trying to get back to work that day. When I caught the train from the station in New Jersey, it took me to Newark. There, I had to catch another train to New York City. Making that connection every day was so much a part of my routine that I typically didn't even think about it. But on that day, I was in such a state of shock that I could not form a connective thought; I could not process words, ideas, or sentences or reason in any fashion. I had known I was pregnant, but it hadn't been real until the doctor said it was real. Now I was in a complete state of dazed blankness.

I remember getting off the train at Newark and standing on the platform. I simply stood there, still as a statue, as other people pushed past me. I had no idea where to go or what to do. I was lost. My mind wouldn't work. Did I go left or right? Did I go downstairs or wait for the train on this level? People were everywhere, and there I stood, growing roots in the concrete. I was suffering from a panic attack, something I had never known before and have never felt since.

Where was I? I had to think. I had to make my legs work. I had to get back to New York. I eventually made it and called him from my office. "Yes," I said. That was it. Just that one word.

"Yes? I'm coming over to your office," he answered quickly.

When we met, he took me in his arms. "I'm sorry," he said. "Are you OK?"

"I am," I answered.

"What do you want to do?" he asked.

"Well, as I see it, we have three choices," I said. "We can get married and have this baby."

"If that's what you want, I'll do it," he said, fear in his eyes.

"Are you in love with me?" I asked.

"No," he answered. Wrong answer, but honest. We were just in the beginnings of a lovely romance. It was too soon to know where it would lead.

"Then what kind of life would we have?" I asked. "I would be trapping you into a life you don't want. We'd end up divorced, and I'd end up raising two children."

"I don't know," he answered in a choked voice.

"The second option is that I have this baby myself, and you help support it."

"OK," he said. I could see his chest constricting and hear the strain in his voice, but he kept his eyes as level as possible and directly on mine. He was a good man, and I could tell he wanted to do the right thing.

"The problem with that choice is that I can barely manage to take care of my daughter and work full-time," I explained. "I'm eking out an existence through sheer willpower, and emotionally, I'm trying to be a mother and father, and it's unfair to Leigh Anne. She deserves all my time, love, affection, devotion, and attention and is hardly getting any of it as it is. I'm knocking myself out trying to make a life for her, and I can't imagine what I'd do with an infant. I can't even picture it. It absolutely terrifies me."

He said nothing but let me speak.

"The last option is to have an abortion," I said. There it was, the dreaded, hateful, sinful word, out in the open. I knew this would be difficult for him too. It hung in the air for a while, like our unborn child dangling by its umbilical cord between us.

"I suppose that makes the most sense," he said. "You completely have the right to make the choice; I want you to know that. Whatever you choose, I will go along with it." Also not a good answer—not "No, no, don't do it!" which was what I wanted him to say.

But he was a decent guy. Really. He would have married me, I think. At least, at that moment, I believe he thought he would. I knew I could not manage a newborn by myself, so that left this other option, the one that everyone hates, the one with the stigma. The one that supposedly God Himself will cast you into hell for even thinking about. Now I had to think about it. Now I had to choose.

"I'm going to have the abortion," I said.

"I'll go with you," he said. And he did.

We went to a very neat, clean little clinic in New Jersey not far from where I lived. He sat with me until they called me into the room where I put on a gown and those funny paper slippers. I went into another room that looked more like an exam room than an operating room. The doctor came in, and we talked. I took some nice medication. Then my legs went up in the stirrups. Nothing to it. It took only a few minutes.

I was resting in another room when he came in. I had just dressed and was having some juice. He had a prescription in his hand, and we walked out together, baby-free. We drove to the pharmacy, and he went inside to fill the prescription for the antibiotics. I looked out the window of the car while I waited and burst into tears. I thought my heart would break from crying. It was, in fact, the first time since the whole thing began that I had let myself feel anything. I cried and cried and choked while I cried. I'd been holding my breath from the moment I found out I was pregnant, and now I could exhale, and with that exhale came all the tears for myself, my daughter, this man, and this beautiful child that I would never know. I cried and cried and cried.

Imagine what he must have felt when he came out of the pharmacy and found me sobbing in the car. He put his arms around me and said, "I'm sorry. I'm so, so sorry!" Then he drove me home and tucked me in bed. He stayed with me for the rest of the day.

We saw little of each other after that. He eventually took another job. It was for the best. Years later, he called, and we had dinner. He'd married a woman with a small child. Funny how life works. The difference was he loved her, and he was happy. Me, I was still single, raising my daughter, and working.

To his credit, he did everything right. He handled the situation exactly the way it should have been handled. He showed grace, consideration, and genuine caring through a difficult time. I'm grateful for that.

When the debate over abortion occurs, I often think of that moment as I stood on the platform at the train station in Newark, in a total state of panic, and of the countless young women all over the world who feel that same panic and will do anything to end their fear. Many of you will never, ever know what it feels like to be in this situation. You can try to imagine it. You can pretend you know what you would do. But if you never have to face it, you have no idea. I understand why a woman would consider doing almost anything to end her unwanted pregnancy. I understand. Panic is sheer fear and adrenaline running through your veins. If you haven't been there, it's easy to think you have a better answer. Logically, you are right. Morally, you are right. Realistically, you are wrong. You will always be wrong.

For a long time, I thought about that child every single day. I wondered what he or she would have looked like, been like— the little boy or girl who might have been tall, with dark hair and sparkling brown eyes like his or her father. I still live with this sadness in my heart. It was consuming then. It has lessened some. I can still tell you each year how old my child would have been. I think about my daughter and all that I robbed her of by denying her that sibling. I have begged God for His forgiveness, but I do not know if He has heard me.

I hate the idea of abortion. I would die fighting for a woman's right to choose it.

This was the ultimate unsuspecting child.

# Twenty-four

*During the summers, with my daughter away, I took acting classes.*
Those rare times when I could explore and exercise and expand
my craft were precious to me. When Leigh Anne returned,
she went back to school, and life resumed its normal pace. But
I missed the theater, so in May 1988, I auditioned for the play
*Summer and Smoke* and was thrilled to be cast as Alma. It would
be my third Tennessee Williams play, after having performed in
both *The Glass Menagerie* (Amanda) and *A Streetcar Named Desire*
(Eunice). The director cast his wife in the lead in *Streetcar*, but
I was happy to play a part and felt that each of these plays was
a gift. Often when I was in a show, Leigh Anne would come
with me to rehearsals and do her homework backstage, and
once the run of the show began, she would clean up the entire
makeup area, organize our costumes, or watch from offstage.

She was the cast mascot, and everyone loved her. Other times, she'd stay at a friend's house for the night.

There is something about a Tennessee Williams play—the slow, southern comfort of the air, the romantic possibilities through love and pain, and the poetry of the words. It's intoxicating.

More often than not, cast members create relationships. Some last; some do not. Once you are out of that arena, the world of reality hits you in the face. I've had some short relationships and some long ones. Whether related to the theater (rarely) or not, some have been good and some devastating, some fleeting and some passionate. Romance always gets me. It's that Disney syndrome again.

One young man took me to a Joan Baez concert because he thought I'd like it (I did like it). I went sailing with another friend who knew my love for the water.

I actually fell in love with a talented man who said I was intelligent and unique and important in the universe. Hearing someone say that they were awed to be worthy of the love they received from me was beyond unusual. It was rare for me to hear romantic words of love, to be touched softly and caringly, to share a bubble bath, or to be given flowers and cheese and wine or cards and kisses.

I experienced a slow kiss so filled with sparks that it turned into a long day of lovemaking and a heated kiss so forceful, so full of fire and chemistry, that in our trying to get to the bed, our clothes ended up on the floor because we couldn't wait those extra few seconds to be together. Sometimes, he'd make me laugh until I couldn't breathe, or we could simply talk about life, art, poetry, politics, the world, and the universe. I thought I had found the answer to what my father had been talking about all of those years ago. But in the end, like every other relationship that I had believed in, there was "goodbye."

They say that a woman wants love, and a man wants sex. They just didn't say that to me back at that time.

One minute you are in love, and the next minute, like a candle on a birthday cake, it goes *poof!*—out in an instant.

Short relationships were easy to get over. Longer ones, where there was hope for a future, finally took a toll and left a hole in my chest where my heart used to be.

# Twenty-five

"*Out with the old, in with the new! MTV!*"

That was the tag line for one of my biggest print ads. I was one of two girls booked for this ad, and we both arrived in our street clothes. We went into the makeup room, and the creative artists went to work on us. The other girl came out looking like the most fabulous model you have ever seen. She had spiked hair and glamorous makeup. Then they put her into a short black dress and spiked heels, and she totally rocked! My hair was teased and sprayed into an enormous flip. I was put into a sexy, long Marilyn Monroe–ish gown and pointy shoes. I stood next to an old black-and-white TV while she stood next to a modern color TV. The ad read: "Out with the old, in with the new! MTV!" Great. My biggest ad, and I ended up being the old broad.

As an avid country music fan, I find there's nothing like

a good "you done me wrong" song to ease a person's aching heart. I got my daughter to become a fan of country music too. Her walking around the house at the age of six singing "Like a vir-r-r-gin, touched for the very first time" seemed inappropriate to me, so I figured she could listen to the stories that country music told and be safer and happier. She fell in love with the Judds immediately, and we sang along to all their songs in harmony.

"Write me a song, Mom," she said.

"What should I write?" I asked her.

She said, "'I'm As Good of a Daddy As a Momma's Gonna Get!'" Good title. I guess my being both a mom and a dad was influencing her, so I took her suggestion and wrote her that song. ("Rock-a-bye and don't cry 'cause I'm here / And I'm gonna wipe away every little tear. / I'll always love you, so please don't forget / I'm as good of a daddy as a momma's gonna get.")

I also wrote one called "Black Hat Cowboy" about the type of guy I always chose ("When it comes to my poor heart / The good guy never wins"). A third song was called "Get a Life!" which was more about my job than anything.

My daughter and I set out for Nashville, and I recorded a demo tape at Don Potter's studio, but he said I had a Broadway voice. I wished the Broadway people thought so! I didn't really know how to market "Daddy," so it sits in a can in my closet. I still think it's a great song.

I was working full-time, auditioning for the theater, performing in soaps and commercials, writing songs, and doing print work. That's a lot of energy spent in a lot of areas. If I could do it again, I'd stick with one thing and keep my eye on the prize.

I was cast in a touring company of *Godspell*. To be able to go, I would have had to send my daughter back to Ohio to live with her grandparents (assuming Mom would even consider it) so that I could chase my dream. I couldn't do it. She was too important to me. I turned it down.

As Leigh Anne got older, she became interested in sports and activities at school. She had friends and studies, and it became clear that I could not continue to do what I was doing and be the mom she deserved. I decided to stop altogether. I wanted to be there for her as much as I could and not miss a minute of it. She already didn't have a father around. Her relatives were far away. She needed her mom full-time. I left Technicolor behind again and went back to black-and-white.

# Twenty-six

*In 1990 one of the partners in the Big Eight firm decided to leave and* merge with another firm that handled a great number of Broadway shows as well as theater, film, and TV stars. He hand-selected several staff members to move with him, including me. At that time, the big firms were merging and would become the Big Four. Wanting to make sure I wasn't dismissed during the mergers, I agreed to go. I was in a new firm, with many of the same people as well as many new people. I was doing taxes for Broadway productions. It wasn't exactly the way I wanted to access Broadway, but I had a child and a responsibility to her.

Within months, I was promoted to manager in the new firm. The managers and senior managers hung out together, going to lunch every day. I was the only woman in the group for a while, and these guys became my closest friends. One day, we went to lunch at a Mexican restaurant, and while we were laughing and talking, Rich, a senior manager, grabbed his napkin and sneezed a huge "Achoo!" into it. He opened up the napkin, and it was full of green, chunky guacamole. I laughed so hard that I thought I was going to pee. This guy was funny! He'd previously seemed like a quiet guy. His wife had passed away, and he was raising a little boy by himself. He was coming out of his shell now, and I found him refreshing. He made me laugh, which I sorely needed.

During the next year Leigh Anne and I moved into a condo, and several of the guys from work came to help. Rich was one of them, and I found him hilarious.

One afternoon I was at home with my daughter and got a call from the bank saying my account was overdrawn. "Not *my* account!" I snapped back. Then I heard laughing. "Is this Rich?"

"Wow, you really got upset," he said with a laugh.

"You're a jerk," I replied.

We began taking our kids out together, just the four of us. We had dinners alone and talked. But mostly we laughed. I was at Rich's house one day when his five-year-old son, Michael, asked if I would come to his room to see his toys. I gladly went with him.

"My mommy is dead," he said.

"Yes, I know. That must be very sad for you."

"We're going to get a new mommy!"

"Oh? Really? And do you have anyone in mind?" I asked.

"Yeah, you!"

Rich asked me to marry him after consulting with the kids first. In 1992, nine years after my second marriage, I took the plunge for the third time.

# Twenty-seven

*The decision to marry again was a difficult one because I was so afraid* of getting divorced. I had regretted being divorced that first time. I had regretted having to do it a second time. I regretted the pain that divorce had caused the men I had once loved. I regretted the pain it had caused my family. I regretted the pain it had caused me. But mostly, I regretted the pain and confusion it had caused my daughter; I had robbed her of a sense of security and family. Getting married again was a huge risk.

I chose to marry my dearest friend, someone I believed would never hurt me. He is a good, decent human being. And he's a very funny person. You have no idea what a joker he is.

Rich hates giving flowers. He thinks it's such a waste of money. Yet on Valentine's Day one year, I came home from work to find a dozen red roses in a vase on the kitchen table with a huge sign: "Happy Valentine's Day. Love, Rich." "You bought me flowers?" I asked excitedly.

My daughter came into the kitchen at that moment, grabbed the sign, and said, "Seriously, Mom?" Under the sign was a small card from the florist that read, "Love, Matt." They had been sent to Leigh Anne from her boyfriend!

"I don't even like you," I said to my husband, who was laughing hysterically. That's him.

But it hasn't always been laughter. It's been a journey, and he's traveled it with me through highs and lows.

Michael needed a mom. Leigh Anne needed a dad. Our relationship was a great opportunity for a new family to come together. It wasn't as romantic as my other dreams of marriage, but it was full of sure, safe, sweet, genuine, loyal friendship. Maybe this was love. Maybe I'd gone about it all wrong before. Maybe it was time to create a real life and stable home for myself, my little girl, this dear man, and his son, whom I immediately legally adopted.

Was this new family perfect? No. Was it fun? Yes. Were there conflicts for my daughter as a stepchild? Yes. It took many years for my daughter and her stepfather to find common ground. There was tension and unhappiness, and more than once my shoes were by the door. That's just who I am—always ready to leave if I have to. I can tell you that my husband and my daughter are now great friends, and he'd battle dragons for her. She's grateful for the family and life he gave her and loves him too. It wasn't easy, but they made it.

Michael was a gift from God. He is now a loving young man. I knew I'd never have another child, so adopting him was more than a blessing. He filled a great part of that hole in my heart. He is as much my flesh and blood as if I gave birth to him. But I always made sure that he knew I was his second mom. His first mom was always a part of his life. Sometimes that was good. Sometimes it hurt. His mom and dad had been very much in love when she died, and she was a tough act to follow.

One of the things I'd done since giving up the stage was start writing. A male friend and I tried our hand at playwriting, and we came up with our first script, *The Other Side of the Rose*. We asked some friends to read and comment on it. They sent us back a tape of the reading of the play, which was a drama, and we could barely hear the lines for the laughter. Evidently, our first effort wasn't that great. Our second attempt, however, was much better. Based on an event from my friend's own life, this play took place in the 1950s and was called *The Jellybean Wars*. We produced the play in the basement of a gay bar in a nearby town. The audience loved the show, and we were thrilled. I'd found a way to stay in the theater, work, and raise my kids at the same time. I knew that playwriting would become a great creative outlet for me. The next play I wrote was for my son and was about his first mom. It was called *Letting Go*.

On our first date with the kids, the waitress had given Michael a helium-filled balloon, and when we got outside, he asked if he could send it to "Mommy in heaven." It was a crystal-clear, blue-sky day. He let go of the balloon, and it went straight up as we all stood and watched it disappear into the sky. I started wondering, *What if she got it?* Rich had a tough time letting go of his first wife. Was she having as difficult a time letting go of this wonderful man and the little boy she'd left behind?

After Rich and I were married, my son said to me one day, "You're nicer than my other mommy." That wasn't good. I asked my husband to tell me why Michael might think that. Something had happened just before his mom passed away that had left my son confused. I thought that if I could write a play explaining what had happened, a play where he could see a real woman playing his mom, telling a real little boy who was playing him that she loved him, it might help.

I set up the stage on two sides. One would be earth, where my son and his dad lived. The other would be his mom's "adjustment" place, where she could see through a "window to the world" what was happening on earth. As they were trying to adjust on earth, she was learning how to let go of life. Meanwhile, the window between them was slowly closing. As I wrote the play, I began to see that there were all sorts of "letting go" issues that I was dealing with in telling this story. Rich's family was having trouble making room for someone new coming into his life (me), I was having trouble with jealousy of someone who was dead (this sainted woman whom they all loved so very much), and my daughter was struggling as well, feeling abandoned by her father over the years, not to mention left out of this new family. I wanted to see if I could write a story that would include all these forms of "letting go" so that we might be able to help other people deal with their own pain.

*Letting Go* was successfully received when it was produced at the Women's Theater of New Jersey in Madison in 1993. Barbara Krajkowski, the director, was totally frustrated with my two-act play and cast of sixteen people, but it was a fair first attempt and got reasonable reviews. (I later rewrote it with a cast of seven.) I was called a "playwright to watch" and "someone who could deliver the goods." We later turned it into a one-act production and produced it off-off-Broadway to good reviews.

I joined the WorkShop Theater, a writer's theater on West Thirty-Sixth Street in New York City. There, I wrote and had two plays produced: *Food for Thought*, which was enormously popular, and *Flight 525*, for our Veterans Festival. I performed in Scott Sickle's play *Demon, Bitch, Goddess*. I was the Bitch, of course. I love these talented friends and artists who drew me into their hearts.

I also had a ball playing a small role in the Gingold Theatrical Group's production of George Bernard Shaw's *The Shewing-Up of Blanco Posnet*, a western! One of my favorite performances was in *'night, Mother*. I played the role of Jessie and could have done that play for years. It was a great way to vent frustration.

It was a great feeling to be back in the theater. I wasn't anyone special or big-time or important, but I was doing what I loved, and I was happy. Most of the time.

# Twenty-eight

For my fiftieth birthday, my daughter and son threw me a surprise birthday party at our home. While my friend Beverly and I went out to lunch and shopped for shoes, my children had all our friends and family come to our home to wait for our return. I was completely overwhelmed (and underdressed) when we arrived to find a house full of people yelling "Surprise!" as I walked through the door. My daughter led me into the dining room, and there, on the large table, she had spread out my life. At face value, I had lived a truly spectacular life. There were the programs from all the plays I had performed in over the years. There were pictures and scrapbooks, reviews and newspaper articles, reprints of advertising campaigns I had modeled for, and copies of scripts I had written that had been produced in both New Jersey and New York City. There were old eight-by-ten glossies from my years of acting and copies of the songs I had written. There was the Chanticleer Award for Best Actress that I'd won for my role as Sally in *Talley's Folly* from a local theater and albums from Up with People featuring songs I had written and recorded. All my union and organization cards were laid out: AEA, ASCAP, AFTRA (not yet known as SAG/AFTRA), and the Dramatists Guild of America.

It was a great party. People took turns standing up and saying lovely and funny things about me and what I had meant to them over the years. There was a lot of laughter, many tears of happiness, and much love in the room. It was a perfect birthday, and I was so proud of my children for giving it to me. After everyone left, I stood looking at that table. I was an actress, a playwright, a singer, a composer, and even, through necessity, an accountant. It was a strange list of ingredients for a life.

But as I took it all in, I knew it meant absolutely nothing. I knew, in fact, that despite how it appeared to everyone on the outside, I had been a complete and total failure.

I was hiding a deep depression and an unending sadness, and I suffered from constant, debilitating flashbacks that I was powerless to stop. Little did I know that things were about to get worse. When confusion meets chaos, the result can be incapacitating.

# Twenty-nine

Rich's first wife had been married before him and had two sons from that relationship. E, as we called him, was the younger of Rich's stepsons and was thirty years old when he came to live with us. When Rich's first wife passed away, both older boys had been devastated. E had been fourteen at the time, and it seemed to me as if he had stopped growing emotionally at that age. By the time he came to live with us, he seemed bipolar, had the emotional maturity of a child, and was full of energy. He loved his guitar, the Beatles, Billy Joel, and the Mets. On these things, he had an unending knowledge of trivia. He never stopped talking, had trouble holding down a job, didn't have a driver's license, smoked weed, and was constantly drinking, crying, acting out, and running up phone bills. I worried about the influence he would have on my son. We talked and talked, and though he listened, he never changed. I tried to get him help by taking him to a clinic for therapy, but since he didn't have insurance, no one would help him. My life was crazy. I was depressed and ready to tell Rich, "Either E goes, or I do." Yet he continued to stay with us for several more years.

Under the surface, my demons were haunting me. My past life was playing out in my mind when my family wasn't looking. They had no idea what was going on; no one did. I was living as two people. There was the happy Marylee that everyone saw, and then there was the person I was in my head. There was the creative Marylee, and there was the responsible one who worked at the black-and-white job each day to earn a living. There was the Marylee who had a zest for life and the one who felt invisible at work, tortured by the mere act of walking into a job that did not fill my soul. There was the Marylee who kept trying to love and had hopes and dreams and the one who had let life slip by with her foolishness. Both Marylees were tormenting each other. I felt pulled to do something bigger, greater, more exceptional than I had ever accomplished. It had always been that way, and the feeling was really starting to take a toll on my emotional well-being.

Sadness permeated my soul. It was a sorrow that lived in my heart and seeped into every happy moment I tried to create for myself and my family. I could not get rid of it, and it was slowly pulling me down into its depths. I had lived a life, but to me it was the wrong life. I felt like I was a sham and that my life was in shambles.

One day, as we were riding along a flat stretch of highway, I asked my husband what he was thinking about.

"Nothing," he said.

"No, really," I replied. "What little things are going through your mind as you drive?"

"I'm not really thinking about anything. I'm just driving," he answered, seeming confused by my question.

Really? He wasn't thinking about anything? I didn't understand. My mind was going all the time, especially when I was looking out a car window. I somehow stopped seeing the scenery, and the movies in my mind began. I started seeing each terrible, abusive thing that had affected my life over the years. Little vignettes replayed over and over, and I caught myself reanalyzing all the things that had happened to me. They were paralyzing me.

Why couldn't I let go of the wretched days in the past? Was I using the bad things that had happened to me as an excuse for not doing something special with the days I had left? Was I so trapped by the fear of failure that I preferred to lie on the ground where it was safe?

People often ask each other, "If you could do your life over, would you change anything?" And I hear the other person say, "No. I would not be who I am today if it were not for all the things that I have lived through." Ask me. *Ask me!* Would I change anything? Absolutely!

I was over at my daughter's house, and as we sat folding laundry, I spoke to her about what I was feeling.

"Maybe you need to talk to someone," she replied. "Maybe it's time for professional help."

That stopped me in my tracks. *What type of person needs professional help?* I thought. *Not me!* I'd been taking care of myself for a long time, yet clearly, I hadn't been doing that great a job. My frustrations, fears, guilt, sadness, and sense of hopelessness were becoming overwhelming, and my daughter, a brilliant young woman with a master's degree in language and speech pathology, had enough background to know it was time for a professional to step in. She didn't know the details of what

I had been through and what I was struggling with, but she knew I was troubled.

She'd always said she had "the most incredible mother in the world." Her mom "could do anything." Her mom "was the best mom." The eight years we'd spent alone together had been difficult years for me. Being both Mom and Dad to her had been an enormous responsibility. I worried about her safety, our finances, whether she was getting love and real care from the people who were watching her when I wasn't around, and whether I was giving her the type of stable home environment she deserved when I was home. I tried to be there for her with dance and gymnastics, cheerleading and volleyball, school trips, and sleepovers at our apartment. I made sure she had fun with friends, had the clothes she needed, got to see shows in New York as well as movies, and was able to go to parties and do all the things kids her age were doing. But had I robbed her of a normal family home? Was she secure in herself? Her grades were great, and she was a fun and funny child, strong and strong-willed. She needed all those qualities to survive the hard life we were leading. I find it so odd that years later, when looking back on that time, she'd say, "I remember those years as the happiest time in my life."

It would be a few years before I got around to it, but I eventually took my daughter's advice and made an appointment with a psychologist. My intention in seeking therapy was to work out the problems that had been going on at home for some time, mostly those involving my stepson. I was in for a surprise. My depression and confusion, my inability to concentrate, and the fog that was always in the back of my head came from a totally different place. It would take two long years of therapy before I discovered that I had lived through an unusual form of child abuse that had sent my life spinning out of control. With the help of a gifted psychotherapist, I went back into my life—way back. Before I could tackle the here and now, I had to understand the roads traveled by the people before me and how their actions had affected my life. What I learned is that much of our inner life has been written in our very DNA. How the people before us lived trickles down through generations and makes us who we are.

# *Thirty*

*On Tuesday, September 3, 2003, I entered the world of psychiatry and* psychology, something I had never known how much I needed.

I sat in the waiting room of a psychiatrist's office, terrified I'd encounter someone I knew. What was I doing? It had taken a long time, many years of screwing up my life, to get to this point. Now I was going to talk to some stranger about my feelings and thoughts? This was a bad idea. How would I start? "Hello. I'm in a bottomless pit." Good. Done. Can I go home now?

I was just about to leave when I heard someone say, "Marylee?" It was the doctor, a petite older woman with a German accent. Think Dr. Ruth. I followed her into her office, where she indicated a seat and shut the door behind me. We talked for about forty-five minutes, and I tried to tell her as much as I could about what I was feeling: hopeless, confused, sad, and lost. I filled her in on my situation at home and my life in general while trying to sound positive and upbeat. I chose a few things to talk about. I could only remember a few things anyway. My mind was a muddle of emotions.

"I passed by you in the lobby," she said, "and I saw that you had very sad eyes. And now here you are, in my office laughing and smiling and telling me your story, and yet still, your eyes are very sad." She continued, "Freud always said that when you have a heaviness here" (she pointed to her heart) "you must get it out here" (she pointed to her mouth), "or it will end up here" (she pointed to her head). "I believe there is a great heaviness in your heart. You need to talk. We will help you. I will assign a therapist for you."

Then she said the dearest thing. "You tell me that you are fifty-three. You do not look fifty-three. You are still young! This is the United States of America! You have many years for happiness!" God bless the United States of America!

She assigned me to a psychotherapist on staff named Donna. I was impressed when Donna called that very evening to set up an appointment. I was not thrilled that she wanted me to fill her in briefly on what was up. I tried to give her a short explanation of what I was feeling. It was hard to go into much detail over the phone. But it gave us a chance to get to know each other a little while I was comfortable in my home and while she was wherever she was before we were closed into the small, cold walls of some office. (Would there be a couch?) She sounded young.

When I finally met Donna, she was about thirty-five, pretty, and sweet. I wasn't sure that such a young woman could help me cope with my devastating past, but I decided to give her a chance. I almost laughed when I walked into her office and saw a couch in the room. I sat in a chair and wondered if

I'd ever find myself lying down on that couch. We chatted for a few minutes, and then she asked, "What brought you to me?"

I had to start now. Where should I begin?

"Well," I said, "I called my doctor and left a message for her: 'Elfie, I'm cracking up. Call me.' She returned my call, and I told her, 'I need twenty-eight days in rehab … except I don't drink, but I can start! I can't sleep. I can't eat. I can't think. I'm crying all the time. I'm in a deep, deep pit, and I can't seem to crawl out of it. I need help.' She agreed and recommended I talk to someone, so here I am."

"Let's touch on some of the things that are bothering you," she said.

And so we began, covering one little thing at a time. We didn't solve much on the first visit. I just began to tell my story. I told her where I was from and what had been happening in my life. Before I knew it, my time was up, and we set another appointment.

And on it went. That first year, we talked about many situations. *We* talked. She was wonderful that way. If I said my husband snored, she would laugh and say hers did too, and we'd talk about that for a while. We talked about our kids. I'd tell her how I was feeling and what I was thinking and why I was hurting. She listened, but she also responded. She was a great listener. She could listen actively for a long time but did not just sit there silently. She would ask questions and steer me into deeper thoughts. And occasionally, one tiny thing she would say after I'd talked for a long time, one tiny comment, would make a light come on in my head, and I'd say, "Really!" I knew I was discovering truths about myself for the first time.

During that first year, even though there were a lot of tears, there were still a lot of walls. I had forgotten so many things. Or perhaps I didn't want to remember them. She told me the movies in my mind were flashbacks. We talked about E and why I couldn't help him. I told her about my crazy youth. We talked about whatever I wanted to talk about. And we solved the problems we could solve.

Then I was done, the first time. I decided, "I can take it from here."

She said, "I'm here if you need me."

E finally moved out, and I felt better for a while, and then I started to realize that we weren't through yet. I still felt full of heartache. I returned to therapy, and Donna and I met again for another year. The process of exploring the mess of one's life takes a long time. There were more areas to work on and stressful subjects to talk about. Walls take a long time to build and a long time to take down when you're doing it one brick at a time. We were deep into the second year of appointments before she finally uncovered the real reason my life had spun out of control. It was a complete shock. It couldn't be true, and yet it made so much sense.

# *Thirty-one*

*That second year, Donna brought my life full circle and found the source* of the bad choices I had made over the years. It wasn't an excuse, mind you, but a reason. She made sense of it all, and the enlightenment gave me such a feeling of wonder and awe and self. I'd give anything to have taken that step toward finding closure and peace when I was twenty-three instead of fifty-three, but taking the step at all was the greatest decision I've ever made, for which I owe my daughter an enormous thank-you.

At the end of my second year of seeing Donna, I had begun to remember almost everything that had happened to me over the years, and I was shaken. The sheer volume of stories I had to tell was astonishing.

"Why?" I asked her. "Why did all this happen to me? Am I marked somehow? Is there a sign on my head?"

What the heck had gone wrong? If I looked back on it, on all the tattered remnants of my life, and wondered about the road I had taken, it seemed there must have been a big arrow pointing at me that said, "Pick her!" Was it easy for people to see? Was it something in my eyes or the way I stood? Were predators lurking out there, waiting just for me? Could predators sense the vulnerability and the weakness? Or had I brought all this on myself? Could I really have been so blind and stupid? What had caused me to repeat the same mistake, over and over, consistently placing myself in the path of danger?

In an episode of the TV show *Two and a Half Men*, Charlie Sheen's character is talking to his roommate about going to a bar. He says, "We'll have to separate the weak from the herd." There you have it. Some of us are seen as easy prey. Our weakness shows in everything we say, the stories we tell, and the way we present ourselves. What had made me so weak? I had to know.

My faith, my hope, and my ability to love, to trust, and to feel were shattered—gone, nonexistent. I was broken. There was nothing left. I had bounced along on my merry way, believing good things were going to happen, and had gladly walked into the wolf's den. The courage and strength I'd thought I had was a sham. I was exhausted from it all and nowhere near where I had intended to go. And where was that anyway?

That's what Donna and I were determined to find out during that final year of therapy. I finally had all the stories—all but one. And then she asked me one simple question, a question she had asked me before but that I had ignored as a possibility. My answer shocked me. It shocked me so badly that I could hardly believe it. And then everything finally made sense.

Donna had asked me many times if my father had sexually

abused me as a child, and I had always said, "No! No way. My father loved me more than anyone in the world, and I loved him. He was always there for me. He photographed my every living moment, recorded my plays, and was my favorite person to confide in. He knew me better than anyone on the planet."

Donna was convinced that there was something in my childhood I wasn't seeing, so during that second year of counseling, she rephrased the question. She turned it, just a tiny bit. "Did your father do anything with you that might be considered strange or unusual?"

I stopped and thought about it. "Well, I guess, maybe," I said.

I told her how it had started when I was nine, after my dad had his affair. We had always talked, Daddy and me. We could talk about anything. But after his affair, we had talked even more. I had become his friend, his pal, his confidante.

I told her how my dad and I would have long talks. I recounted how he had told me about his affair in detail and had talked about how Mom was unresponsive and frigid. I recalled how he'd said that the church wouldn't permit birth control, and to Mom, that meant sex was for procreation. I told Donna how he'd gone into detail about sex and wanted me to be a better, more perfect wife someday. I explained that he had just wanted me to know what my sexual responsibilities were. The stories came tumbling out.

The difference between Dad and Mom when they discussed sex with me was the way they looked at the matter.

Mom had been raised in an orphanage by a group of nuns, had been deserted by her father, and had never, ever talked to us about any of it. We knew little about Mom's background. When explaining sex to me, Mom had said, "The man's penis becomes erect. He places it into the woman's vagina, and semen comes out. This semen travels up to meet with an egg produced by the woman, and hopefully, it fertilizes the egg, and a baby is made."

Dad, on the other hand, said, "The force of a man's drive is extremely powerful. Once it's started, it can be harmful to a man to stop it. During sex, the man's penis is hard and full, and an explosion takes place when the semen is sent out into the woman's uterus. That's when the fertilization of the egg occurs."

Dad was always more visual in his descriptions of sex. He was certainly unhappy in his sexual relationship with Mom. Often, he'd pour out his frustration with Mom to me. He told me every detail of their married sexual life in the most graphic manner. He described their encounters so that I might understand what was wrong with them and learn from them.

"Sex should be a long, enjoyable experience," he would say. It clearly was not for him. Mom wanted it over with quickly. He tried to explain how I should behave as a wife, how I should keep my husband happy and give my husband pleasure. He told me never to pretend and explained how important it was not to satisfy myself too quickly and to make sure that my husband was satisfied. He told me, "Take care of how you look, how you dress, how you present yourself so that your husband is attracted to you."

It wasn't a single big conversation. It was many conversations over many years, until I was eighteen and ran away with the circus, or in my case, the musical. He wanted his daughter to be perfect. I wanted to be perfect too. I wanted to make my dad proud of me. I wanted to be a wonderful wife. I was just a young girl, but I was an avid pupil. I was going to make my husband happy. I wasn't going to make him sad and miserable. I couldn't understand why my mother wasn't making my father happy. All she had to do was relax, enjoy herself, give in, and do the things he was telling me about. I knew that I would be a fabulous wife, and I was going to be good at sex.

"If you keep a man satisfied sexually, he will never want to stray or leave you," my father said.

I listened carefully. He never touched me. There were lots of hugs and fatherly kisses. I sat on his lap or held his hand as we talked, and I didn't think it was unusual that he was talking to me in this way. I liked being his confidante. I felt special and important. He wasn't talking with my sister like he was with me. He wasn't giving her "special" advice. There was no one for him like his "little girl," and he told me so, all the time.

He told me that after sex there should be a warm cuddling time, where you lie together, stroke each other, and enjoy the rapture. But Mom, he said, would jump up immediately and run for the bathtub. "Maybe she doesn't like the semen running down her legs," he informed me.

I made a mental promise not to mind the mess and always to cuddle afterward.

My father also filled me with confidence. He was thrilled with my talent onstage. He loved to hear me sing. He always told me how proud of me he was. "There isn't anything you can't do if you just set your mind to it," he'd say. "I believe in you. God gave me a gift when He gave me you. I'm the luckiest father in the world."

I believed him. He was the standard I held all other men up to. He was my hero. He loved me unconditionally, and he told me so all the time. "I'll always love you, no matter what." He created the structure of my life and my identity, and I held his hand while it happened.

Even when I was an adult, he would make strange comments that were meant to show me his love. "I should have married you!" he had said one evening while standing naked in an open bathrobe. In response, I just rolled my eyes and walked away. It hadn't really seemed all that important, just a little odd.

Then Donna spoke the three words that would change my life. "What happened to you is called mental sexual incest."

It had a name. The term hung in the air like a dark cloud.

And then, all at once, the cloud lifted, the haze cleared, and *boom! Boom! Boom! Boom! Boom!* The doors opened in my mind, and my whole life made sense.

I went from shock to anger, to rage, to wonder, and then to sorrow for this little girl with the big eyes and blonde curls who had listened with such an open heart, hoping that by learning how to be good enough sexually, she might be worthy of being loved one day.

It was a setup, Dad.

I was so angry with him! How could he do that to me? I wanted to take a bat into the backyard and hit the heck out of a tree. I wanted to take a head of lettuce and stomp on it.

About a month later, I was taking a shower, scrubbing my hair furiously, and I started to cry. I knelt on the floor of the shower and sat there and sobbed until I couldn't cry anymore. I let the steaming-hot water pour over my body and wash the shame away. It was done, out of my head at last.

# $\mathcal{T}$hirty-two

*We were going back to Ohio for a family get-together, and I decided to* ask Dad about what had happened. He owed me. He was in his eighties, and though he was using a walker, his mind was clear. He was sitting in the living room, quietly reading, when I sat down beside him.

"Can we talk, Dad?" I asked.

"Of course," he said sweetly.

"Dad, remember those talks we used to have when I was little? Remember how you taught me all about sex and being a good—"

"Let's see what's on TV," he said, and he quickly turned on the TV at full volume.

I knew then that we would never have that talk. There would be no healing or apologies. It was over.

I told Rich, and he gave me a big hug. "You've done what you could. Now just heal yourself," he said wisely.

My father passed away in 2012. I sat beside him and held his hand while he died. My sister was recovering from breast cancer at the time. My friend Cam and my cousin Denise were with me. Mom passed away two years later. She had battled Alzheimer's for ten years. I was in New Jersey, but my sister sat beside her as she passed.

My stepson E passed away in September 2010 at the age of thirty-six. He had a heart attack related to alcohol poisoning. I blamed myself for not having been able to save him.

I don't believe my father intentionally meant to harm me. In fact, I think it would have broken his heart to know the havoc his secrets had wrought on his little girl's life. And yet it is undeniable that the road to my destruction began there, when I was a small child wrapped in the arms of the one man who was supposed to protect me and bring me through childhood safely.

Later, I was told of another term, "covert incest." I looked it up. As described in Wikipedia, "Covert incest, also known as emotional incest, is a type of abuse in which a parent looks to their child for the emotional support that would normally be provided by another adult. The effects of covert incest on children when they become adults are thought to mimic actual incest, although to a lesser degree. This term describes interaction[s] by a parent and child that are exclusive of sexual abuse." I understand that actual incest is worse, but I'm not sure I agree with the term "lesser." It is still horrific. Dr. Kenneth Adams, author of *Silently Seduced*, said, "Typically the parent is motivated by loneliness and emptiness of a troubled marriage so he or she turns the child into a surrogate partner." That certainly fit my dad.

I heard this term again on Leah Remini's award-winning TV series *Scientology and the Aftermath*. Dr. Natalie Feinblath, a psychologist appearing on the show, said, "Overt sexual abuse involves touching. Covert sexual abuse does not involve anybody touching anybody. When a child is exposed to pornography or people having sex or sexually explicit conversations, that can be completely inappropriate for a child, that can be just as damaging as overt sexual abuse." That was really validating.

Whatever you call it, Dad, it really messed me up.

You were the one man I knew loved me totally and without question.

So I spent the rest of my life believing that if I was good enough in bed, if I was sexually attractive and could keep a man interested, someone would want me. If I failed sexually, then I failed as a woman. A relationship between a man and a woman was all about how the woman performed in bed or how the woman looked, or a man wouldn't want her. Simple as that. This idea was embedded in my brain from the time I was a small girl, and it was the thing I tried to focus on to make every relationship I ever had work. I wasn't old enough or savvy enough to get it, so I failed at it. How can you be good at sex when you have so much going on in your head while you're doing it? I learned early that sex was a bad thing (the Catholic Church said it was a sin if you weren't procreating), but Dad said that a woman should learn to be great at sex and let her husband do it often (because her husband would love her for it), and she shouldn't stop him, or it would hurt him. I learned all sorts of techniques (from him and from the guy who was supposed to be my teacher). I never learned a thing about love.

I was blind as a bat. If I had spent as much time focusing on being an actress as I had trying to be loved, I'd have had a tremendous career. And I might have learned that relationships are about people and feelings, passions and interests, common goals and communication.

The sadness that permeated my very existence, the insecurity, the need to be liked, and the desire to be loved created such confusion in me that I mistook, misjudged, and misinterpreted every relationship I was a part of.

I came to believe later, as my body began to wear out from abuse, stress, anxiety, and regret, that any physical pain I suffered was God paying me back for the life I had led. Surely God hated me. God was saying that I had to live in pain as a punishment for my sins. When I fell off a ladder while painting the ceiling of my dining room before my daughter's wedding, I was sure God was punishing me for the horrific life I had led. The migraines I suffered all my life were surely God's way of telling me how disappointed He was with me. I was paying for my sins, and I had committed so many. But could I suffer enough pain in my life to earn the right to enter eternity when I died? I didn't think so. I would be damned to the eternal blazes of hell forever.

I had prayed to God so many times over the years. I had begged God to help me. I had cried for His love and guidance. It was hard to believe in God. It was hard to believe in His forgiveness. So many times, I had believed that things would be all right if I just asked God for help. And so many times, someone would come out of nowhere and knock my lights out when I least expected it. My faith was shot. How could anyone save my shattered soul?

I knew it wasn't God's fault.

It was what it was. I was a little girl who was "preconditioned" at a very young age, a young girl whose mind was filled with images and thoughts that would form her values when she was most impressionable, long before she was old enough to experience any of these things. When I should have been thinking about the carefree things that kids think about, my mind was full of concerns about the adult world of marriage and sexual encounters. It was not a matter of blame. It was a matter of knowing and, in knowing, understanding.

That was when it finally hit me. That was when I realized the most important part of this discovery. I found some peace in the idea that one thing was certain:

I could have taken no other path.

# Thirty-three

*Donna had identified the source of my pain.*

Even as an adult, I would have continued down the same path without professional help. I am free now. If you are dealing with something similar, I want that freedom for you.

I once saw a doctor because I had been experiencing fatigue and muscle pain, and I couldn't figure out why. During the exam, the doctor asked me, "Has anything traumatic happened in your life? Sometimes stress or a past traumatic event can create this kind of thing."

Was he kidding? I said, "No."

Some of the people I talk about in the pages of this book were or are people I love. Many have passed away; some are still around. But this story is about the children out there who, for whatever reason, are suffering from abuse, overt or covert. Two victims, Wade Robson and James Safechuck, heartbreakingly discuss their survival of alleged sexual abuse by the iconic superstar Michael Jackson in the 2019 documentary *Leaving Neverland*. Their journey into sexual abuse certainly began covertly. They became friends with Michael, then became special friends, then were told that what he felt for them was love. What began covertly for them soon became overt sexual abuse. In watching the documentary, I was completely awed by these two young men. Speaking their truth took phenomenal courage. The truth of abuse spoken aloud can be both healing and terrifying. The look of pain in their eyes hit home. That pain takes years of hard work to lessen. These men both continued their lives; they have had successful careers, and they married and had sons of their own while the demons in their heads were crushing their spirits. They are a real example of unsuspecting children, drawn into a horrific situation and believing they were special and loved. They have taken the ultimate risk in speaking out in order to find peace of mind. I hope they find it and will be free.

In her follow-up television broadcast *After Neverland*, Oprah Winfrey said, "This moment transcends Michael Jackson. It is much bigger than any one person. This moment in time allows us to see this social corruption. It's like a scourge on humanity. It's happening in families; we know it's happening in churches and in schools and sports teams everywhere." This abuse involves, as Oprah said, "grooming a child" through "a slow, gentle, kind, loving care that makes him or her feel extraordinarily special." Listening to these words, I was shocked at how often abuse starts with the words "I love you." This love is felt so intensely that "anything and everything the person with whom they are involved does is all about love. It is a certainty; they do not consider that it could be anything else." Oprah gets it, and she opened my eyes to how easy it is for a child to be swept into a devastating relationship without ever seeing the devastation ahead.

Plus, it's always a secret. I understand that deep obligation to protect someone you love who has professed to love you so much. I hope those people who have been abused and whose stories have come to light in this way will continue their therapy and find their way out of the past.

Therapy can be a life-changing tool. For me, it was the beginning of my road back. Accepting my truth was a long and difficult process, but it was worth every moment. It was the start of letting go of all the things that had happened to me. They are part of who I am, but they no longer define me. They happened. I cannot change them. They make sense now. Did they make me who I am? Unfortunately. Can I live with that? Yes. All the demons are out now. They have a connection. I understand why I did what I did and how it all came to be.

I forgive my father for his foolishness. He needed a friend. So did Mom. I understand her so much better now. She came from such a difficult background and thought she had found the man of her dreams. Instead, she found herself on the outside of my father's family, a group that did not really accept her. Then Dad had his affair, and the whole family took his side with only one exception: my sister. She adored Mom and stood by her. But even having Kathy on her side, Mom must have felt so alone and betrayed. Her anger toward the father who had deserted her, possibly toward the mother who had put her in an orphanage for years, and then toward Dad and his family must have been spirit-breaking.

Mom may have always seemed mad or upset, yet I know she loved us enough to jump in front of a speeding car for us. She would have benefited from serious counseling. She could have been free. She deserved happiness more than any of us.

She got the brunt of my dislike in ways she never deserved. She held our family together, she stood by her husband for sixty-six years, and even as her own sickness began, she waited on him hand and foot when he became disabled later in life. She was underappreciated and misunderstood.

I love you, Mom. I'm so sorry.

I'm sure God understands that the little girl with the earnest heart just wanted to be loved as she made her many mistakes. He's like that.

I can see her clearly now, that unsuspecting child, for who she was, and I forgive the mistakes she made as a result of what she endured. I also forgive those who made mistakes with her along the way.

I let my sister see an early draft of this book, and she was astounded at what had transpired under our roof without her having an inkling. This information did, however, answer her questions about why Dad and I had been so close and why she had never felt that same connection with him. We have held on tightly since then and will never let go of each other. We could have been friends. At least now we are loving sisters.

Sharing this story with all of you has been hard for me. Perhaps some of you will say, "I would never bare my past like that for the whole world to see. Why risk it?"

I'll tell you why I did it. I did it for one reason.

# Thirty-four

*I have shared my story here for the woman (or man) who has been* through this kind of abuse. I wrote this book for those people who need help, for people who are living in confusion, fear, and sadness, with a lack of self-esteem and flashbacks that won't stop.

I did it for you.

It can happen to anyone. There have been so many successful, spectacularly talented, and remarkable people who have ended their lives by suicide as a way to escape their pain. Some of my friends can't seem to find it in their hearts to feel compassion for these people. "They're rich! They're famous! They have everything! What do they have to be depressed about? Try our lives!"

The demons in our heads are not deterred by money or

fame. Depression is a kidnapper who will tell you lies and steal you away.

I was lucky. Really.

When I first started writing this, it wasn't a book at all. Donna said, "You have all these feelings and stories. You're a writer. Write them down."

So I did. I didn't begin writing a play or a novel or even a book. I just wrote down the events, one at a time, just to get them out of my head. Then, somewhere in the middle of it all, I started thinking about you—you out there with your scars that still hurt, spinning out of control, lost in the woods like I was, trying to navigate your own path. That's when I thought, *Maybe I'll risk it, for you.*

The story of *An Unsuspecting Child* is my story, from my point of view and my memories as I recall them. My daughter never would have put up with the crap I took from men. She'd have knocked them flat. My son would never treat a woman that way; I raised him not to. As children they knew only the happy mommy who loved them. Only when I fell into the hole, after stumbling around blindly and lost all those years, did I discover the effects of my past. By then, the compassion of my children was greater than I could have expected or felt I deserved.

I know there are survivors of abuse who bear visible scars, but for many others our scars are hidden deep inside. The current #MeToo movement is giving a voice to these survivors. I applaud the continuing courage as more women come forward.

For those of us who were abused as children, let's get rid of our shame or self-blame and say, #WeeToo! I want you to know that you too are warriors and victors in the eyes of those who bear the invisible scars of abuse. I know it hasn't been easy for you. It's not easy for anyone.

Let me leave you with these words: There is no shame in anything that's happened to you. What would be a shame is if you don't grab this chance to live every day of your life as fully and happily as you can.

You are beautiful.

You have a voice. Speak out.

You have an inner voice. Listen to it.

You have animal instincts. Obey them.

You deserve happiness.

You are not guilty of anything.

You have the right to get these demons out and to be free.

I love my children. My beautiful, intelligent, creative daughter and my fabulous, funny, affectionate son are more precious to me than ever. Do I understand love now? It's not at all what I thought it was going to be. It's not what I read about as a child. It's not what my dad said it should be.

As I am writing this, we are in the midst of the COVID-19 pandemic. As of June 11, 2020, there had been over 7.4 million cases worldwide and over 417 million deaths worldwide reported as COVID-related. We are constantly quarantining ourselves, wearing masks, and staying home. The economy has plummeted. From March through June, our daughter and daughter-in-law taught virtually while their own children went to school virtually. Michael and Rich have been working remotely from our townhouse, and I'm writing in the bedroom to keep out of their way because the loft and dining room table are covered in tax returns.

The presidential election has caused huge tension in our home. Rich is Republican; I am a Democrat. The differences in our views have affected us more than they have during any other election.

Racial unrest is at an all-time high, and I feel like we are back in the sixties all over again.

Climate change has been pushed to the side, and the world seems to be shouting at us to pay attention as fires, dust storms, and hurricanes constantly threaten us.

Will this marriage survive? Tomorrow is never promised. I'm taking it one day at a time.

Am I great at sex? I've had my moments. It hardly seems to matter with everything else that's going on. Yet I still hear my father's voice in my head, telling me it's the only thing that matters. What I've learned is that intimacy isn't about sex as much as it is about warmth, togetherness, and understanding. Intimacy takes many forms. Sex is just one of them.

Who am I really? I've had a lot of names. There is my maiden name and all those married names that have come and gone. Marylee Martin is the name I chose as an actress. I wasn't any of those other people anymore. I was the girl who had run away to a city where no one knew who she was. I was an actress with no past. No one cared. I liked it that way. I like that name. No one can take it away from me.

I was sitting in the back of a golf cart, riding around Sarasota, Florida, and my girlfriend's husband, Steve, was sitting beside me. He'd asked to read the book, and I thought a male's opinion might be helpful. He mentioned all the traveling I had done, the plays I had been in, the plays I had written, the songs I had recorded, and the work I had done as a tax accountant. I told him that I had spent most of my life feeling like an impostor. While the partners in the accounting firm had always treated me with respect, my peers had looked down their noses at me. They had degrees. They were better than I was, and they knew it. I was a second-class citizen and endured their disdain for thirty-three and a half years, even though I was entrusted with one of the largest returns our firm prepared. I was nothing to them.

Steve looked at me and said, "Are you kidding? You have a PhD in life experience!"

My daughter always thought I was looking for fame. She didn't realize that what I was looking for was acknowledgment, assurance of my self-worth, respect, achievement, acceptance, and accomplishment. And yes, Technicolor.

I still suffer from loneliness, even when I'm with a group of people. I still have a deep insecurity that will not go away. I still make sure to put my makeup on after my shower. I'm constantly refreshing my lipstick. Once, while going to Ohio, I switched places with Rich so I could drive for a while. Just as I was about to go down the ramp onto the highway, I suddenly pulled over.

"What's wrong?" Rich asked.

"I forgot to put on my lipstick!"

Some things are so ingrained in my system that I cannot get rid of them.

I still wish my life were different, even though I'm as happy as I will ever let myself be. My life isn't perfect, so I remind myself that no one else's life is perfect either. I try to memorize happy moments and replay them, filling up that space in my head with joy. I replay Christmas Day when the kids were small and we had a house full of relatives. Some were on the couch, some sat on the stairs, some rested in comfy chairs, and kids sat on the floor near the tree. I can hear the talking and laughing as we passed out gifts. I see the paper flying and the children shrieking with excitement. Nothing could be any better than those moments.

I'm retired and busier than ever, writing, traveling, spending time with my grandchildren, and looking forward to whatever lies ahead. The future is full of possibilities.

The damage done at the start, unrealized and compounded, could have been stopped by self-awareness and the realization that I had, like Dorothy in *The Wizard of Oz*, the power all along to change my destiny.

So do you.

# Acknowledgments

Somehow, the words "thank you" hardly seem enough. Nevertheless, thank you to Donna, a wonderful psychotherapist and wizard. You saved my mind, my heart, and my life, and I am forever grateful to you for being there and magically lifting me out of the well.

Thank you to Janet Boros for editing the first draft of my book, to Kevin Anderson and Associates for editing the second draft,and Pat Sellers for tearing it all apart, asking hard questions and preparing it for another look.

Thank you to everyone at Archway Publishing for your dedication, professionalism, and encouragement throughout the publishing of this book. Your thorough inspection and care have been amazing. I am so grateful for all of you.

To Johnny Montagnese, owner/producer at the Carriage House Studios in Stamford, Connecticut, thank you for your professionalism, friendship, and laughter during the audio recording of this book.

Special thanks to John Gonzalez for being my memory in the details of traveling with Up with People.

To friends who read, commented on, and supported this project: Kathy, Glenda, Steve, Debbie, Cam, Heather, Lizbeth, and Denise, thanks for your input.

Thank you to Emily Alpert at Elliportraits for a fun, highly professional day of getting a photo suitable for this book.

I'd like to thank my husband, Rich, for offering me moral support and understanding while I wrote this. It's been quite a ride over the last twenty-eight years. You've been amazing!

Thank you to my son, Michael, for his support and for being my tech guy!